JOHN BEVERE

Devotional Workbook

Extraordinary

The Life You're Meant to Live

Extraordinary Devotional Workbook
Copyright © 2009 by Messenger International

Published by: Messenger International, P.O. Box 888, Palmer Lake, CO 80133-0888
All rights reserved. No portion of this book may be reproduced, stored in a retrieval system, or transmitted in any form or by any means—electronic, mechanical, photocopy, recording, or any other—except for brief quotations in printed reviews, without the prior permission of the publisher.

Unless otherwise noted, Scripture quotations that are unmarked (or marked NKJV) are taken from the NEW KING JAMES VERSION.
Copyright © 1979, 1980, 1982 by Thomas Nelson, Inc. Used by permission. All rights reserved.

Scripture quotations marked AMP are taken from the AMPLIFIED® Bible.
Copyright © 1954, 1958, 1962, 1964, 1965, 1987 by The Lockman Foundation. Used by permission. (www.Lockman.org)

Scripture quotations marked CEV are taken from the CONTEMPORARY ENGLISH VERSION®.
Copyright © 1995 by American Bible Society. All rights reserved.

Scripture quotations marked KJV are from The Holy Bible, KING JAMES VERSION.
Copyright © 1970 by Thomas Nelson Inc.

Scripture quotations marked NASB are taken from the NEW AMERICAN STANDARD BIBLE®.
Copyright © 1960, 1962, 1963, 1968, 1971, 1972, 1973, 1975, 1977, 1995 by The Lockman Foundation. Used by permission. (www.Lockman.org)

Scripture quotations marked NIV are taken from the HOLY BIBLE: NEW INTERNATIONAL VERSION®.
Copyright © 1973, 1978, 1984 by International Bible Society. Used by permission of Zondervan Publishing House. All rights reserved.

The "NIV" and "New International Version" trademarks are registered in the United States Patent and Trademark Office by International Bible Society. Use of either trademark requires the permission of International Bible Society.

Scripture quotations marked NLT are taken from the Holy Bible, NEW LIVING TRANSLATION.
Copyright © 1996. Used by permission of Tyndale House Publishers, Inc., Wheaton, IL 60189. All rights reserved.

Scripture quotations marked The Message are taken from THE MESSAGE.
Copyright © 1993, 1994, 1995, 1996, 2000, 2001, 2002. Used by permission of NavPress Publishing Group.

Scripture quotations marked TEV are from TODAY'S ENGLISH VERSION.
Copyright © by American Bible Society, 1966, 1971, 1976, 1992.

Scripture quotations marked TLB are taken from THE LIVING BIBLE.
Copyright © 1971 by Tyndale House Publishers, Wheaton, IL 60187. All rights reserved.

Unless otherwise noted, italics and bold treatment used in Scripture, Voice of the Ages, and Fascinating Facts indicate the author's added emphasis.

WRITTEN AND EDITED BY:
Vincent M. Newfield
New Fields & Company
P. O. Box 622 • Hillsboro, Missouri 63050
www.preparethewaytoday.org

COVER, INTERIOR DESIGN & PRINT PRODUCTION:
Eastco Multi Media Solutions, Inc.
3646 California Rd.
Orchard Park, NY 14127
www.eastcomultimedia.com

Design Manager: Aaron La Porta
Designer: Heather Huether

Printed in Canada

Table of Contents

Quick Overview and Suggestions for Use IV

Chapter 1: God's Pleased with Extraordinary 1

Chapter 2: Revealed as We Are 15

Chapter 3: You Can Do It! 29

Chapter 4: Newness of Life 45

Chapter 5: Holiness 61

Chapter 6: The Kingdom Within 79

Chapter 7: The Access 95

Chapter 8: Beyond Comprehension 111

Chapter 9: True Faith Is Relentless 127

Chapter 10: What Are You Listening To? 143

Chapter 11: The Flesh 159

Chapter 12: God's Imperial Rule 175

Helpful Tips to Make the Most of Your Extraordinary Journey

Welcome to the *Extraordinary* Devotional Workbook! We're excited and honored you have chosen this curriculum. The in-depth study you hold in your hands, along with John's dynamic book and video and audio teachings, pack the potential to revolutionize your life!

Much prayer and research have been invested in creating this interactive study. It contains 12 chapters that directly relate to the 12 teaching sessions. Each chapter is crafted from one or more chapters in the *Extraordinary* book and consists of a series of revealing questions and an inspiring devotional, along with a place to "Journal Your Journey" of growth each week.

YOU'LL ALSO BE EQUIPPED THROUGH FEATURES LIKE...

- **Heaven's Appeal** – life-transforming words from Scripture. We encourage you to take time to meditate on the message of these passages that contain the power to transform your life.

- **Voice of the Ages** – timeless truths from heroes of the faith. Be open to receive direction and wisdom from these pioneers who have blazed the trail before you.

- **John's Quotes** – Power statements from the book and teaching series that emphasize and reinforce the core theme of each chapter.

- **The Bottom Line** – a concentrated overview of the entire lesson, encapsulating the highlights and insights you'll want to remember.

Along the way, you'll also discover several fascinating facts, important definitions, and a special section of scripture references for further study. Everything has been prayerfully selected to help you apply these principles, teaching you how to unveil your hero!

Be sure to write down any personal thoughts, feelings, ideas or insights the Holy Spirit reveals to you in the **journal** and **notes** sections at the conclusion of each chapter. The scriptures and principles that come alive and explode on the inside of you are divine treasures to cherish. This will help you grow spiritually and is well worth investing the time to jot down for future review.

We also suggest you...

- **BEGIN AND END WITH PRAYER.** With each session, invite the Holy Spirit to teach you and guide you into all truth (see John 16:13). As you complete the chapter, ask Him to permanently seal in your heart what you have learned.

- **READ THE RELATED CHAPTERS** in the *Extraordinary* book, watch or listen to the teaching, and then complete the session in the devotional workbook.

- **PACE YOURSELF** to complete each chapter during the week or allotted time. You may do it as part of your daily routine or work on it two or three nights a week. Remember, there is no right or wrong way to do it; this is your *personal* study with the Lord.

- **BE CONSISTENT & COMMITTED.** Whatever time and place you choose to do your study, stick to it. If you fall behind, don't quit. *Press on* to the end. God will faithfully bless your every effort.

- **BE HONEST** with yourself and God as you answer each question. Knowing the truth of God's Word and the truth about yourself will bring freedom to your life that can be found no other way.

Remember...

> ...The measure [of thought and study] you give [to the truth you hear] will be the measure [of virtue and knowledge] that comes back to you— and more [besides] will be given to you who hear.
>
> **—Mark 4:24 AMP**

So give yourself wholeheartedly to this 12-week course. Be open to what your heavenly Father wants to do in your life. There are many questions that will more than likely be answered as you saturate yourself in the truths that are presented. Before you begin, pray this prayer with us:

Lord, grant me a spirit of wisdom and revelation [of insight into mysteries and secrets] in the [deep and intimate] knowledge of You. Flood the eyes of my heart with light, so that I can know and understand more fully the hope to which You have called me, and how rich is Your glorious inheritance in all the saints. Thank You for teaching me and equipping me to live extraordinarily...in Jesus name, Amen!

[based on Ephesians 1:17-18 AMP]

No eye has seen, no ear has heard, and no mind has imagined what God has prepared for those who love him.

—1 Corinthians 2:9 NLT

xtraordin

God's Pleased with Extraordinary

Please refer to chapters 1, 2 and 3 in the *Extraordinary* book, along with session 1 of the teaching series.

> Your life is *unique*, *special*, and by no means an accident. No one is common, no one is menial; we were created for the *extraordinary*. Each of us has a unique path that God has prepared for our lives.
>
> **JOHN BEVERE**
> adapted from chapter 3

Extraordinary *vs.* ORDINARY

Extraordinary means "beyond what is usual, customary, or ordinary; exceeding the common measure; remarkable, rare, wonderful."[1] Words synonymous with "extraordinary" include amazing, exceptional, and special. The opposite of "extraordinary" is *ordinary*, meaning "common, average, mundane, usual, or normal."

1. Unlike any other part of creation, men and women are created in the image of God. We are "godlike," meant to reflect His extraordinary nature—prospering, reproducing and taking charge of the earth (see Genesis 1:27-28 The Message).

    a. When you hear the word *extraordinary*, what images and feelings come to mind?

    _____

    _____

    _____

    _____

    _____

    b. Which people in your life would you say live extraordinarily? Why?

_____

_____

_____

_____

c. Of all the extraordinary men and women in the Bible, whom do you most admire and/or connect with? Why?

_____

_____

_____

2. As you begin this journey discovering the extraordinary life God has planned for you, take a few moments to evaluate your thoughts on being a Christian.

a. Describe the current image you have of Christianity.
(Be honest; there's no wrong answer.)

_____

_____

_____

_____

_____

_____

b. Who or what specific things (circumstances, experiences) have helped form this image?

_____

_____

_____

_____

_____

3. Satan, the god of this world and archenemy of both God and us, masterfully manipulates the world's system and all those who are *not* born again and belong to God. One of his primary purposes is to paint a picture showing that God's people are *not* extraordinary.

Voice of the Ages

"If conversion to Christianity makes no improvement in a man's outward actions—if he continues to be just as snobbish or spiteful or envious or ambitious as he was before—then I think we must suspect that his 'conversion' was largely imaginary; ...A tree is known by its fruit; or, as we say, the proof of the pudding is in the eating. When we Christians behave badly, or fail to behave well, we are making Christianity unbelievable to the outside world. The wartime posters told us that Careless Talk Costs Lives. It is equally true that Careless Lives Cost Talk. Our careless lives set the outer world talking; and we give them grounds for talking in a way that throws doubt on the truth of Christianity itself."

—C.S. Lewis[2]

a. Of all the things that frustrate Satan, what does he probably fear the most about you being a Christian? (See page 5 in the book.)

_____

_____

_____

b. **Write out** the related power principle found in 1 Peter 2:9. Personalize it by replacing the word *you* with *I* (or me) where appropriate.

_____

_____

_____ 1 Peter 2:9

4. In the days of the early church, Christians were held in high esteem by society, even viewed by some as gods. Today, however, Christians are often viewed in a negative way—especially in America.

a. What do you think it will take for Christians to once again be held in high regard and recover the respect the early church had?

_____

_____

_____

_____

_____

_____

_____

_____

Heaven's APPEAL

Even as [in His love] He chose us [actually picked us out for Himself as His own] in Christ before the foundation of the world, that we should be holy (consecrated and set apart for Him) and blameless in His sight, even above reproach, before Him in love. His unchanging plan has always been to adopt us into his own family by sending Jesus Christ to die for us. And he did this because he wanted to!

—Ephesians 1:4-5

[verse 4 taken from The Amplified Bible; verse 5 from The Living Bible]

b. Is there anything specific God is showing you that needs to change in your life to see this happen? If yes, what is it?

_____

_____

_____

_____

5. Read and *meditate on the message* of the following scriptures about God's love:

> ...then the world will know that you (*God the Father*) sent me (*Jesus Christ*) and will understand that **you love them as much as you love me.**
>
> **John 17:23 NLT**
>
> But **God shows and clearly proves His [own] love for us** by the fact that while we were still sinners, Christ (the Messiah, the Anointed One) died for us.
>
> **Romans 5:8 AMP**
>
> (*God's*) love bears up under anything and everything that comes, **is ever ready to believe the best** of every person, its hopes are fadeless under all circumstances, and it endures everything **[without weakening].** (*God's*) love never fails [never fades out or becomes obsolete or comes to an end]...
>
> **1 Corinthians 13:7-8 AMP**
> [italic words in parentheses added for clarity]

a. What do these verses say to you personally about God's love for you? How does your disobedience or sin affect His love for you?

_____

_____

_____

b. What kinds of *thoughts*, and consequently *feelings*, does the enemy bring against you to try and downplay God's love and make you believe He doesn't love you or loves you less than others?

_____

_____

_____

_____

c. Through what specific ways (or experiences) has God clearly communicated and proven His deep love for you?

_____

_____

_____

_____

> Never doubt the love God has for you. It's *not* conditional; it's not based on your *performance*, or how good you've been. It's a constant love that never fades out or comes to an end. If you would have been worth one cent less to God than the value of Jesus, then God wouldn't have sent Him to die for you; for He would never make an unprofitable deal! In God's eyes, *Jesus' value is the same as yours!*

JOHN BEVERE
adapted from chapter 2

6. Who does Jesus Christ esteem (value) *more*—you and others, or Himself? Explain what He has done that backs this up. (See Philippians 2:1-8 and Romans 12:10.)

_____

_____

_____

_____

7. The Bible has a lot to say about God's plan of salvation and what it cost Him to restore us back into right relationship with Himself. (See 1 Peter 1:18-19.)

   a. Read Colossians 1:12-14 and 2 Corinthians 5:17 and explain what happens in your life and in the realm of the spirit when you sincerely surrender yourself to Jesus.

   _____

   _____

   _____

   _____

   b. Briefly explain God's superior plan of salvation for man, including why Jesus had to be both 100 percent God and 100 percent man. (See page 15 in the book.)

   _____

   _____

   _____

   _____

Check out John 3:16; Ephesians 2:8-9; and Romans 3:23; 6:23; 10:9. It is valuable for you to know in your heart God's plan of salvation, not only for yourself but also for the sake of sharing it with others.

> "A remarkable, amazing, extraordinary life is not restricted to certain individuals or professions. It doesn't matter who you are or if you're a school teacher, businessman or woman, government leader, stay-at-home mom, athlete, factory worker, hairstylist, student, pastor, or anything else. God has called you and created you for the extraordinary *in that role.*"

JOHN BEVERE
adapted from chapter 1

Heaven's
APPEAL

Cheerfully pleasing God is the main thing, and that's what we aim to do, regardless of our conditions.

—2 Corinthians 5:9
The Message

8. While God's love for us is unconditional, unchanging, and never-ending, pleasing Him is another story. Although we can't do one thing to make Him love us any more or any less than He already does, we are *personally responsible* for how pleased He is with us.

a. The power to live extraordinarily and please God is not based on your occupational position. What is it based on? (See page 4 in the book.)

_____

_____

_____

_____

b. If you live with the supreme goal of pleasing God, what two things can you expect to happen in your life? (See page 13 in the book.)

_____

_____

_____

9. One of the main motivations to please God is knowing that each of us will one day stand before Him and give an account for what we have done with our lives (see 2 Corinthians 5:10 and Romans 14:12).

a. As a believer, what will you be judged for when you stand before God? How does this motivate and challenge you?

_____

_____

_____

_____

_____

_____

Check out Ecclesiastes 12:14; Jeremiah 17:10; 1 Corinthians 4:5.

SALVATION ≠ ETERNAL REWARDS

"What we do with the cross of Jesus Christ indeed determines WHERE we'll spend eternity; however, *the way we live* as believers determines HOW we'll spend it."

JOHN BEVERE
adapted from chapter 3

10. Just as heaven is a real place, so is hell. It is also referred to as Gehenna, Hades, Sheol, Eternal Fire, the Pit, the Abyss, the second death and place of everlasting punishment. The subject of hell is actually mentioned in the New King James Version more than 154 times—18 by Jesus Himself.

Heaven's APPEAL

So do not make any hasty or premature judgments before the time when the Lord comes [again], for He will both bring to light the secret things that are [now hidden] in darkness and disclose and expose the [secret] aims (motives and purposes) of hearts. Then *every man will receive his [due] commendation from God.*
—1 Corinthians 4:5 AMP

a. Countless people have asked, "Why would a loving and merciful God send men and women to hell?" If you were asked this question, how would you answer it?

_____

_____

_____

_____

_____

the bottom line

God has created **you** to live a truly extraordinary life of purpose and fulfillment. He loves you with an everlasting, unconditional love and has equipped you to carry out specific plans on the earth. When you live extraordinarily, you please Him and His plans for your life are revealed and fulfilled.

GOD'S PLEASED WITH EXTRAORDINARY

UNVEIL YOUR HERO

...kicked out of school
for asking too many questions

Thomas Edison–Inventor

Journal Your Journey

...work out (cultivate, carry out to the goal, and fully complete)
your own salvation with reverence and awe and trembling
(self-distrust, with serious caution, tenderness of conscience,
watchfulness against temptation, timidly shrinking from whatever might
offend God and discredit the name of Christ).
—Philippians 2:12 AMP

EYE-OPENERS

As you have gone through this week's study on living an extraordinary life
and pleasing God, what eye-opening revelation(s) of truth has the Holy Spirit
made real to you that you had never seen before?

REVOLUTIONARY YOU

God always wants us to mature and come up higher in our way of living.
How is He challenging you to change your way of thinking and acting to better exemplify His extraordinary character? What *new goals* is He prompting
you to set in your life?

Voice of the Ages

"What is my task? First of all, *my task is to be pleasing to Christ*. To be empty of self and be filled with Himself. To be filled with the Holy Spirit; to be led by the Holy Spirit."

—**Aimee Semple McPherson**[3]

You Mean EVERYTHING to Him!

"For I know the plans I have for *you*," says the Lord. "They are plans for good and not for disaster, to give you a future and a hope."
—Jeremiah 29:11 NLT

God has an extraordinary life planned for you—not average, mediocre, or boring. It was established in the mind of God *before* you were ever born, before the creation of the earth itself. This truth is made incredibly clear in Psalm 139. Look at what David writes...

O Lord, you have searched me and *you know me*.
You know when I *sit* and when I *rise*; you perceive my
  thoughts from afar.
You discern my *going out* and my *lying down*; you are
  familiar with *all* my ways.
Before a *word* is on my tongue you know it completely,
  O Lord.

My frame was not hidden from you when I was made in
the secret place. When I was woven together in the depths
of the earth, your eyes saw my unformed body. All the days
ordained for me were written in your book before one of them
came to be.

Psalm 139:1-4,15-16 NIV

God is amazing! He knows every thought *before* you think it, every word *before* you speak it. He knows when you lie down and when you get up, and He is totally aware of every day of your life before it takes place. With a heavenly Father like this, why go anywhere else for wisdom and direction?

How can you tap into the infinite wisdom of the One who created the heavens and the earth? Through a close, ongoing relationship with Him. He loves you with an everlasting love and wants to be a part of every area of your life. As you read His Word and spend time with Him in prayer, He will reveal to you His general will and His specific will for your life.

"There is a book written about you. God wrote your life out the way He desired you to live it before you were even born. In that book, God set goals for you. Our responsibility is to find out in prayer what His goals are for our personal life and go after them."

JOHN BEVERE
adapted from session 3

Heaven's APPEAL

...we have always prayed for you, ever since we heard about you. We ask God to fill you with the *knowledge of his will*, with all the wisdom and understanding that his Spirit gives. Then you will be able to live as the Lord wants and will always do what *pleases* him. Your lives will produce all kinds of good deeds, and you will grow in your knowledge of God.

—Colossians 1:9-10 TEV

Do you want to know God's will for your life? Do you need wisdom and direction every day? Your heavenly Father wants to give it to you. Read and meditate on the following scriptures and write out what the Holy Spirit speaks to your heart:

Proverbs 3:5-6 • Psalm 25:9,12 • Psalm 32:8 • James 1:5

_____
_____
_____
_____
_____
_____
_____
_____
_____
_____
_____
_____
_____

At this point in your life, what has God revealed about His *specific will* for you? *Get quiet before the Lord* and ask Him to show you any new direction He desires you to take. Write what He reveals.

Heaven's APPEAL

For we are God's [own] handiwork (His workmanship), recreated in Christ Jesus, [born anew] that we may do those good works which God predestined (planned beforehand) for us [taking paths which He prepared ahead of time], that we should walk in them [living the good life which He prearranged and made ready for us to live].

—Ephesians 2:10 AMP

What seemingly impossible God-sized, God-willed goals has He *already accomplished* through you? What are you presently pursuing and believing Him to accomplish through you in the days ahead?

_____

_____

_____

_____

_____

_____

_____

Voice of the Ages

FOR FURTHER STUDY
GOD HAS THOUGHTS
& PLANS FOR YOU
    Psalm 40:5; 139:16-18
    Proverbs 16:9; 19:21
    Jeremiah 29:11

AIMING TO PLEASE GOD
    Proverbs 16:7
    Hebrews 13:16
    1 Thessalonians 2:4; 4:1-12
    1 John 3:21-24

"If we are saved and sanctified, God guides us by our ordinary choices, and if we are going to choose what He does not want, He will [give us a] check, and we must heed. *Whenever there is doubt, stop at once.* Never reason it out and say—'I wonder why I shouldn't?' God instructs us in what we choose, that is, He guides our common sense, and we no longer hinder His Spirit by continually saying—'Now, Lord, what is Thy will?'"
—Oswald Chambers[4]
[words in brackets added for clarity]

1. *Noah Webster's First Edition of an American Dictionary of the English Language* (1828), Republished in facsimile edition by Foundation for American Christian Education (San Francisco, CA 1995). 2. C.S. Lewis, *Mere Christianity* (New York, NY: Macmillan Publishing Co., Inc, 1977) pp. 161-162. 3. Quotes by *Aimee Semple McPherson* (www.quotesea.com/Quotes. aspx?by=Aimee+Semple+McPherson, retrieved 3/5/09). 4. Oswald Chambers, *My Utmost for His Highest* (Uhrichsvillle, OH: Barbour Publishing, Inc., MCMXCVII) p. 155.

NOTES

Investigate my life, O God, find out everything about me; cross-examine and test me, get a clear picture of what I'm about; see for yourself whether I've done anything wrong— then guide me on the road to eternal life.

—Psalm 139:23-24
The Message

Revealed as We Are

2

Please refer to chapters 3 and 4 in the *Extraordinary* book, along with session 2 of the teaching series.

> " Jesus will examine our labor of love and reward us accordingly. However, the believer's judgment will go deeper than our labor, actions and spoken words; the investigation will go to the core of our being—to our *innermost thoughts, motives, purposes,* and *intents.* "

JOHN BEVERE
adapted from session 2

MOTIVE

The word "motive" implies an *emotion* or *desire* (or need) operating on the will and causing it to move or act a certain way.[1] Other words for "motive" include purpose, reason, cause, incentive and drive.

1. Our *motives* mean a lot. They are the "why" behind what we do and are birthed within our *inner man*—the place where we first and foremost please God and where extraordinary living begins.

   a. Read Mark 2:8, Luke 12:2-3, and Hebrews 4:13. What common thread of truth concerning our inner man is found in all these verses? What does this say to you?

   _____

   _____

   _____

   _____

   Also **check out** Psalm 26:2; Proverbs 16:2; 17:10; 23:23.

   b. According to James 4:2-3, what is the result of praying with the *wrong* motives?

   _____

   _____

   _____

15

c. Read Philippians 2:3 and write what it speaks to your heart.

_____

_____

_____

Heaven's APPEAL

...we are constantly ambitious and strive earnestly to be *pleasing* to Him. For we must all appear and be **revealed as we are** before the judgment seat of Christ, so that each one may receive [his pay] according to what he has done in the body, whether good or evil [considering what his *purpose* and *motive* have been, and what he has achieved, been busy with, and given himself and his attention to accomplishing].

—2 Corinthians 5:9-10 AMP

2. As a human being, you have three images: a *projected* image, a *perceived* image and an *actual* image.

a. Briefly explain what each image means.

Projected Image

_____

_____

_____

_____

Perceived Image

_____

_____

_____

Actual Image

_____

_____

b. Which image of you does God *always* see? Which one do you tend to focus on and live out of most?

_____

_____

_____

c. How does *having* or *not having* the fear of the Lord affect the image you live out of?

_____

_____

_____

> *The fear of the Lord* puts God in His place of preeminence. A lack of the fear of the Lord reduces God down to an image made by man.
>
> When you fear God, you know that everything is open and exposed before Him to whom we must give an account. "

JOHN BEVERE
adapted from session 2

3. According to Colossians 1:15 and Hebrews 1:3, Jesus was the visible, expressed image of God the Father. In the same way, the ultimate aim of being a Christian is for you to become the visible, expressed image of Jesus.

   a. It's so important that you **re**present Christ to others—that you *present Him again* in all that you do. Read 2 Corinthians 5:20 and write what it means to you and how you can make the most of your post as an ambassador for Christ.

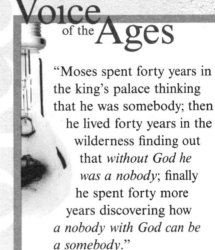

Voice of the Ages

"Moses spent forty years in the king's palace thinking that he was somebody; then he lived forty years in the wilderness finding out that *without God he was a nobody*; finally he spent forty more years discovering how *a nobody with God can be a somebody*."

—**Dwight L. Moody**[2]

   _____
   _____
   _____

4. Read John 2:23-25. Notice that after Jesus did many miracles in Jerusalem during the Passover, many people believed in His name and entrusted themselves to Him. However, Jesus *didn't entrust Himself* to them.

   a. Why did Jesus *not* entrust Himself to others? What do you think He knew about human nature that prompted Him to guard Himself?

   _____
   _____
   _____

   b. What does this say to you personally?

   _____
   _____

Heaven's APPEAL

...You're here to be light, bringing out the God-colors in the world. God is not a secret to be kept. We're going public with this, as public as a city on a hill. If I make you light-bearers, you don't think I'm going to hide you under a bucket, do you? I'm putting you on a light stand. Now that I've put you there on a hilltop, on a light stand—shine! Keep open house; be generous with your lives. By opening up to others, you'll prompt people to open up with God, this generous Father in heaven.

—Matthew 5:14-16 The Message

c. Flattery—our flesh loves it, but receiving it can be deadly. Describe a situation in which you received the deadly deceit of flattery and what you learned as a result.

_____

_____

_____

_____

_____

_____

_____

_____

_____

FASCINATING FACT: A DEADLY DECEPTION

Years ago, Paul Harvey described how an Eskimo kills a wolf. He first coats his knife with animal blood then allows it to freeze. He later adds another layer of blood and lets it freeze. This process is repeated until the knife is completely concealed by the frozen blood. The Arctic hunter then fixes his knife to the ground with the blade facing up. The unsuspecting wolf senses the blood and begins to lick the frozen blood. His appetite for more blood increases with each lick. He begins to lick more vigorously and unknowingly starts slicing his own tongue on the razor sharp knife. The wolf then continues to satiate his thirst for blood with his own warm blood. His perpetual desire will not be satisfied until death overtakes him. In a similar way, the deception of a flattering tongue is deadly. It's packaged in an attractive way but always contains the lethal blade of destruction.[3]

5. The greatest danger of living out of your *projected image*—being overly concerned with what others think of you—instead of your *actual image* is that you become a prime candidate for *deception*.

   a. Read James 1:22-25 and explain how we deceive ourselves. What must you do to avoid being deceived?

   _____

   _____

   _____

b. *Meditate on the message* of Hebrews 4:12-13 and, in your own words, explain how the Word of God transforms you.

_____

_____

_____

_____

_____

Heaven's APPEAL

My enemies cannot speak a truthful word. Their deepest desire is to destroy others. Their talk is foul, like the stench from an open grave. Their tongues are filled with flattery.

—Psalm 5:9 NLT

6. *God's Word* is a spiritual mirror we look into to see ourselves as we really are. It helps us have a healthy fear of the Lord, which keeps us in touch with our actual image and keeps the mirror of the Truth before us.

a. Read 2 Corinthians 3:18 and describe the greatest result of regularly looking into the mirror of God's glory.

_____

_____

b. Who or what in your life also acts as a spiritual mirror? How do they challenge you to be like Christ?

_____

_____

_____

"Here is the sad fact: If we choose to focus on our *projected image*, we will forsake the blessing of being changed into the image of Jesus Christ. We will be deceived and incapable of pleasing God and living an extraordinary life. A person who is deceived believes with all their heart they are right, when in actuality they are wrong. That's scary!"

JOHN BEVERE
adapted from chapter 4

FASCINATING FACT: CHRISTIAN CHAMELEONS
There are approximately 160 known species of chameleons. Most of them have the ability to change their skin color. Research indicates that they do not typically change their color for reasons of camouflage, but instead use color changes as a method of communication, including *making themselves more attractive* to potential mates.

When a person is described as a *chameleon*, the comparison generally refers to their ability to blend into various social situations, often meaning the person has no true values, or that he quickly abandons them in company if it's convenient to do so. Ask yourself: *Do I change my personality and appearance with ease, morphing into a seemingly different person whenever I deem it necessary? Am I a chameleon?*[4]

7. John tells a sad but true story of a man he met on the beach who was a "Christian chameleon." Normally he blended in with the world, but he had the uncanny ability to promptly project an image of a Christian when it was convenient and profitable.

   Get quiet before the Lord and ask yourself these soul-searching questions:

   a. In what ways, if any, am I a Christian chameleon?

   _____

   _____

   b. Do I tend to hide my Christian witness around certain people and blend in with the world? If so, who is it and why do I do it?

   _____

   _____

   c. Which is more important to me: pleasing my friends, family, co-workers, etc., or pleasing God? Why is this the case?

   _____

   _____

   _____

8. Without question, an ongoing and ever-growing *fear of the Lord* is one of the most valuable things we could ever have in our lives.

   a. In your own words, briefly describe what the fear of the Lord is and explain how it is different from being *afraid of God.*

   _____

   _____

   _____

   _____

Voice of the Ages

"To please God even a little is infinitely greater than to have the acclamations of all our race throughout the centuries."

—**Charles H. Spurgeon**[5]

b. What are some of the benefits of living with a healthy fear
of the Lord? What does the fear
of the Lord protect you from?

_____

_____

_____

_____

_____

Check out Exodus 20:20; Psalm 25:12; 31:19; 103:13; Isaiah 8:11-14a.

Heaven's APPEAL

The *fear of the Lord* is the
beginning of wisdom; a good
understanding have all those
who do His commandments...
—Psalm 111:10 NKJV

"**You will serve who you fear.** If you fear God, you'll obey God. If you
fear man, you'll ultimately obey man's desires. Many times it is harder
for us to offend the person we see—especially if we desire their love
and friendship—rather than the One we don't see."

JOHN BEVERE
adapted from chapter 4

9. Moses had an indelible encounter
with God at the burning bush; it
implanted the fear of the Lord into
his heart and changed his life
forever.

a. Take a few moments and tell of
a time when you had an indelible encounter with God, and
explain how it has changed
your life forever.

_____

_____

_____

Voice of the Ages

"It is only the *fear of God*
that can deliver us from
the fear of man."
—John Witherspoon[6]

10. What do you think is the current condition of the church in the western
world? Is there evidence of a lack of the fear of the Lord? If so, list some
of the common causes for this in the church.

_____

_____

_____

_____

Heaven's APPEAL

All has been heard; the end of the matter is: **Fear God** [revere and worship Him, knowing that He is] and **keep His commandments**, for this is the whole of man [the full, original purpose of his creation, the object of God's providence, the root of character, the foundation of all happiness, the adjustment to all inharmonious circumstances and conditions under the sun] and the whole [duty] for every man. For God will bring every deed into judgment, including every hidden thing, whether it is good or evil.

—Ecclesiastes 12:13-14

[verse 13 taken from AMP; verse 14 from NIV]

_____

_____

_____

_____

_____

A Prayer for Your Pastor and Church Leaders

Lord, thank You for my pastor and church leaders. I pray that the fire to valiantly proclaim the pure truth of Your Word would persistently burn bright in their spirits. I ask that You give them a holy boldness to continually walk in the fear of the Lord and not the fear of man... in Jesus' name, Amen!

the bottom line

God knows all and sees all, including the true motives behind your every action. An ongoing awareness that you will one day give an account of your life to God will help keep your motives pure and develop a healthy *fear of the Lord*. This heartfelt reverence is also established and maintained by listening to and obeying God's Word. As you live your life with the goal of *pleasing God*, you'll be free from the snare of the fear of man and the danger of deception.

UNVEIL YOUR HERO

An everyday couple adopts a teenage foster child and rescues twin boys from the severe poverty of Haiti.

Aaron & Tanya's capacity continues to be enlarged...

Journal
Your Journey

" Rise up, leader! Rise up, Christian! Our God is calling you to make a huge difference in our generation. We've been called to go against the grain of the spirit of this age, the spirit that works in the sons of disobedience, the spirit of this world. We've been called to bring heaven to earth! "

JOHN BEVERE
adapted from chapter 4

EYE-OPENERS

As you have studied this week's session on identifying the real you and living in truth, what eye-opening revelation(s) has the Holy Spirit made real to you that you had never seen before?

REVOLUTIONARY YOU

In what specific ways is God challenging you to change your way of thinking regarding the fear of the Lord and the fear of man? What *new goals* is He asking you to set in relation to time in His Word and not pursuing the approval of others?

PRAYER

Father, thank You for loving me. I ask You to forgive me for doing things out of impure motives and being more focused on pleasing others than pleasing You. I repent for being a "Christian chameleon" at times, trying to win the approval and praises of others. Wash me clean from the inside out; give me a fresh hunger for Your Word and a deep desire to not just hear it but do it. Develop a healthy fear of You in me, and give me the desire and strength to build a good reputation for You and bring You glory...in Jesus' name, Amen!

REPUTATION
It's *NOT* About You

> Let this mind be in you which was also in Christ Jesus, who,
> being in the form of God, did not consider it robbery to be
> equal with God, but **made Himself of no reputation**,
> taking the form of a bondservant, and coming in the likeness
> of men. And being found in appearance as a man,
> He *humbled* Himself and became obedient to the
> point of death, even the death of the cross.
> —Philippians 2:5-8 NKJV

Many people in the world today are fighting fiercely to climb the ladder of success. A great deal of their energy is focused and spent on building a reputation in the eyes of others in order to "make it big." In the process of their pursuit, they quickly become addicted to the approval of others.

Jesus did just the opposite—He *made Himself of no reputation* (Philippians 2:7). In other words, He stripped Himself of all His kingly rights and humbled Himself to become human. The Creator literally took the form of His creation. Instead of living His entire life to build a name for Himself, He endeavored to build a name for His Father. He said, "...I am not in search of honor for Myself. [I do not seek and am not aiming for My own glory.] There is One Who [looks after that; He] seeks [My glory], and He is the Judge" (John 8:50 AMP).

Read Genesis 11:1-9. How did God respond to the people who were driven to "make a name for themselves"? What does this say to you personally?

_____

_____

_____

_____

Jesus was sinless, perfect and went about doing good everywhere He went (see Hebrews 4:15; 1 Peter 2:22). Yet, people criticized Him and slandered His name. What does this say to you about your name, even when you do good to others?

_____

_____

_____

_____

MEDITATE on the MESSAGE...

Don't lose your grip on Love and Loyalty. Tie them around your neck; carve their initials on your heart. Earn a **reputation** for living well in God's eyes and the eyes of the people.
—Proverbs 3:3 The Message

A sterling **reputation** is better than striking it rich; a gracious spirit is better than money in the bank.
—Proverbs 22:1 The Message

And he must have a good **reputation** with those outside the church, so that he will not fall into reproach and the snare of the devil.
—1 Timothy 3:7 NASB

Interestingly, Proverbs 3:3-4, 22:1 and 1 Timothy 3:7 encourage us to develop a good reputation. What type of reputation is this referring to, and what is the value of having it?

_____

_____

_____

_____

According to Matthew 5:14-16 and 1 Peter 2:11-12, how do you bring glory to God in the world?

_____

_____

_____

_____

Voice of the Ages

"Humble yourself and cease to care what men think. A meek man is not a human mouse afflicted with a sense of his own inferiority. Rather, ... he has stopped being fooled about himself. He knows well that the world will never see him as God sees him and he has stopped caring. He has obtained a place of soul rest. The old struggle to defend himself is over."
—A. W. Tozer[7]

Heaven's APPEAL

It is dangerous to be concerned with what others think of you...
—Proverbs 29:25 TEV

If our actions are motivated by the *approval of others*, we are focused on our projected image. As a result, we will often be led to act like a hypocrite just like Peter did with the Jewish leaders in Jerusalem (see Galatians 2:11-14).

Get quiet before the Lord. Be honest as you answer these questions:

How important is my reputation, or standing, in the eyes of others? Why?

_____

_____

_____

Who do I try to impress by my actions? Why is their approval so important to me—what's motivating me?

_____

_____

_____

> "God spoke to me one day and said, 'John, the moment you seek to please people is the moment you forsake your calling—you will no longer be a servant of Christ; you will be a *servant of man.*' Now don't get me wrong: As a servant of Christ, I serve men. But what God is saying is, **'Don't be in bondage to men's opinions.'**"
>
> **JOHN BEVERE**
> adapted from session 2

FOR FURTHER STUDY

FEAR OF THE LORD
Psalm 19:9; 112:1-3; 128
Proverbs 1:7; 9:10-11; 10:27
Proverbs 14:26-27; 15:16,33
Proverbs 16:6-7; 19:23; 22:4
Isaiah 8:12-14

FLATTERY & MOTIVES
Psalm 26:2-4
Proverbs 16:2; 28:23
Romans 16:17-18
Philippians 2:3
1 Thessalonians 2:3-6

FEAR OF MAN
Psalm 27:1-3; 56:4,11
Romans 8:31
Isaiah 51:12-13
Jeremiah 1:8,17
Hebrews 13:6

NOTES

1. Adapted from definition of *Motive* (www.merriam-webster.com/dictionary/motives, retrieved 3-11-09). **2.** Quotes by *Dwight. L. Moody*, (www.dailychristianquote.com, retrieved 3-10-09). **3.** Raymond McHenry, *McHenry's Quips, Quotes & Other Notes* (Peabody, MA: Hendrickson Publishers, Inc. 1998) adapted from p. 65. **4.** Adapted from definition of *Chameleons* (http://en.wikipedia.org/wiki/Chameleon#As_a_metaphor, retrieved 3-11-09). **5.** Quotes on *Pleasing God* by *Charles Spurgeon* (www.spurgeon.us/mind_and_heart/alphalist.htm#m, retrieved 3/5/09). **6.** Quotes by *John Witherspoon*, see note 2. **7.** Quotes by *A.W. Tozer*, see note 2.

We have *everything* we need to live a life that pleases God. It was all given to us by God's own power...

—2 Peter 1:3 CEV

xtraordin

You Can Do It! 3

Please refer to chapters 5 and 6 in the *Extraordinary* book,
along with session 3 of the teaching series.

> "We have everything it takes to live a life that pleases our heavenly Father.
> So settle this in your heart and don't ever let this knowledge slip away.
> God is the One who spoke these words through Peter. His Word is true and
> unchangeable. Never, at any time, accept the lie that you don't have
> what it takes to please God. The fact is that you do!"
>
> **JOHN BEVERE**
> adapted from chapter 5

1. No matter how difficult it may have been (or is) to please your *earthly*
   father or mother, you have what it takes to please your *heavenly* Father.
   God Himself has given you the ability!

   a. What kind of behavior, achievements, etc. do you feel God expects
      from you?

      _____

      _____

      _____

      _____

   b. *Get quiet before the Lord.* Read your answer from the previous
      question aloud in prayer and ask the Lord to confirm in your heart
      what He really expects from you.

      _____

      _____

      _____

      _____

Heaven's APPEAL

...he has told you what he wants, and this is all it is: to *be fair*, *just*, *merciful*, and to *walk humbly* with your God.
—Micah 6:8 TLB

2. The parable of the minas and the parable of the talents are actually *not* one and the same. The biggest difference between them is that in the parable of the minas everyone was given an *equal* amount, and in the parable of the talents each was given *different* amounts.

a. In the *parable of the minas*, what does the mina represent? Give some practical, real-life examples of the "minas" God has given you.

_____

_____

_____

_____

b. In the *parable of the talents*, what does the talent represent? Give some practical, real-life examples of the "talents" God has entrusted to you.

_____

_____

_____

_____

c. What do you believe God wants you to do with the "minas" He has given you? How about the "talents"?

_____

_____

_____

_____

Check out the parable of the minas in Luke 19:11-26 and the parable of the talents in Matthew 25:14-30.

" A person's ability to write, teach, preach, sing, compose music, design, manage, organize, lead, interact well with people, and so forth are all gifts given by God. If I keep that in mind, it guards me from the deadly traps of pride and envy. Pride, in thinking I'm better than others; envy, in coveting what another person has. "

JOHN BEVERE
adapted from chapter 5

3. According to Ephesians 4:7 TLB, "...Christ has given **each of us** special abilities—whatever he wants us to have out of his rich storehouse of gifts." These special abilities, or gifts, are His *grace*. *Meditate on the message* of the following scriptures and answer the questions that follow:

> ...A man can receive nothing [he can claim nothing, he can take unto himself nothing] except as it has been granted to him from heaven. [A man must be content to receive the *gift* which is given him from heaven; there is no other source.]
>
> **—John 3:27 AMP**
>
> Who made you superior to others? Didn't God give you everything you have? Well, then, how can you boast, as if what you have were not a *gift*?
>
> **—1 Corinthians 4:7 TEV**
>
> ...Every desirable and beneficial *gift* comes out of heaven. The gifts are rivers of light cascading down from the Father of Light...
>
> **—James 1:17 The Message**

a. Have you ever desired a gift or ability that someone else had? What was it? In a way, what are you saying to God when you covet what someone else has?

_____

_____

_____

b. Have you ever measured your success with someone else's? How did it make you feel? Did God speak to you about it?

_____

_____

_____

c. How do these verses shed new light on *comparing* and *competing* with the gifts in others?

_____

_____

_____

Heaven's
APPEAL

For it is by free **grace** (God's unmerited favor) that you are *saved* (delivered from judgment and made partakers of Christ's salvation) through [your] faith. And this [salvation] is not of yourselves [of your own doing, it came not through your own striving], but it is the gift of God; not because of works [not the fulfillment of the Law's demands], lest any man should boast. [It is not the result of what anyone can possibly do, so no one can pride himself in it or take glory to himself.]
—Ephesians 2:8-9 AMP

4. As John Newton's ageless hymn declares, God's grace is truly amazing! Not only is it amazing, it is also *multifaceted*. Read Ephesians 2:8-9 and, in your own words, explain what it means to be *saved by grace*.

_____

_____

_____

_____

_____

_____

_____

_____

_____

_____

_____

5. Many people from all walks of life and religious backgrounds are struggling to *earn* their salvation and entrance into heaven by the works they do. Even many Christians, after they get saved, attempt to stay in God's good graces by being "good enough." (See Isaiah 64:6.)

a. In what ways, if any, have you fallen into the trap of trying to maintain right standing with God through good behavior?

_____

_____

_____

_____

_____

Voice
of the Ages

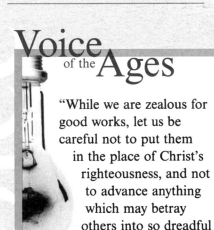

"While we are zealous for good works, let us be careful not to put them in the place of Christ's righteousness, and not to advance anything which may betray others into so dreadful a delusion."
—**Matthew Henry**[1]

b. Read Galatians 3:1-9; 5:4 and share what the Lord shows you about constantly trying to *work your way* into right relationship with Him or earn His blessings.

_____

_____

_____

> "When we are at the judgment seat before God and He looks at us and says, 'Why should I admit you into My kingdom?' our answer will not be because we lived a good life or because we worked hard in ministry or because we touched people's lives. It will be purely because of what Jesus did at the cross of Calvary—shedding His blood, dying, being buried and being raised to life again! That amazing ransom that was paid by His life is what saved us—*nothing else*."
>
> JOHN BEVERE
> adapted from session 3

FASCINATING FACT: SAVED BY GRACE

Billy Graham has ministered to people throughout the world for five decades. He has preached to over 110 million people in 84 countries. In addition to these who have heard him in person, he has been heard by countless others through radio and television. Three million people have responded to his invitation to receive Christ or make a recommitment. There is no question that Billy Graham has made a significant impact for Christ. Yet, all of these efforts will not gain him entrance into the presence of Christ. *Every person is saved by the grace of God*, not good works (Ephesians 2:8-9).[2]

6. While we were still sinners, God's grace was given to us in the form of *saving grace. Meditate on the message* of the following scriptures and explain what the Holy Spirit reveals to you about the different aspects of God's saving grace.

Acts 15:11 • Romans 3:21-24; 5:14-17 • Titus 2:11-12; 3:4-7

_____

_____

_____

_____

_____

_____

_____

7. Have you ever done something that seemed so awful you thought for sure you lost your salvation? You're not alone; most believers have experienced this one or more times in their lives.

a. Briefly explain a situation like this in your life and how God brought you out of it.

_____

_____

_____

Check out 1 John 1:9, Acts 13:38 and Ephesians 1:7 for a glimpse of His heart toward you.

b. Read Romans 6:1-2, Galatians 5:13 and 1 Peter 2:16 and explain the one thing you should *never* do with the freedom of God's grace.

_____

_____

_____

_____

_____

Voice of the Ages

"Where would any man or woman be this very hour were it not for the **grace of the Lord Jesus Christ**? Grace greater than all our sins—grace greater than all our shortcomings.

I am reminded of God's grace when someone confides, 'I wasn't worthy of this healing or of God's blessings. I am not worthy to be called an heir of God and a joint-heir with Christ Jesus.'

It isn't a matter of being worthy, for no man is worthy! It isn't our perfection or our penitence, or a matter of our labors to reach the place of perfection or worthiness. *It is God's grace alone!*"

—Kathryn Kuhlman[3]

Heaven's APPEAL

O my soul, bless God. From head to toe, I'll bless his holy name! O my soul, bless God, don't forget a single blessing! He forgives your sins—every one...
—Psalm 103:1-3 The Message

8. When it comes to forgiveness, it is a great encouragement to know that God will forgive us of anything we've done wrong when we humbly confess it to Him. In the same way, He requires us to forgive others.

a. In Jesus' discussion with Peter about forgiveness in Matthew 18:21-22, what is He actually saying about how often we are to forgive others? Why should it be this way?

_____

_____

_____

_____

_____

Check out Matthew 6:14-15 and Ephesians 4:32.

MERCY

The Hebrew word for "mercy" is *hesed* or *chesed*. It describes not just the emotion of pity, much less the ignoring, excusing, or indulging of wrongdoing; it implies *kindness* and *compassion* and that one can be depended on to faithfully carry out the promises made in a covenant or agreement. By this, God "[kept] covenant and mercy" with His people, the Jews, in terms of showing loyalty to them—even when they didn't deserve it. In the same way, God calls those who fear Him to show mercy in their dealings with others.[4]

9. God's *extraordinary* forgiveness is inseparably linked to the richness of His grace and *mercy*. As Psalm 136 overwhelmingly declares, His mercy and love endure forever! In the same way, He commands us to extend mercy to others. (See Luke 6:36.)

a. Briefly share a situation in which you were shown mercy and how it impacted your life.

_____

_____

_____

_____

_____

_____

Hint: Think back to past situations with teachers, coaches and your parents.

b. Whom do you feel God is asking you to show mercy to but you would rather not? Why is it hard for you to do?

_____

_____

_____

_____

Pray and ask the Lord for grace to give mercy to those who need it, just as He has given it to you.

FASCINATING FACT: GRACE & PEACE TO YOU!

In all of the Apostle Paul's epistles, he starts by greeting his readers with "grace" and "peace." Why did he use these two words so frequently? First, he used them because he was an apostle to the Gentiles, or Greek-speaking world, and it was necessary for him to greet his Greek readers in their customary way. During New Testament times, the salutation of "grace" was the customary greeting exchanged between Greeks when they came near each other. Just as we say, "Hello, how are you doing?" as a polite way of greeting someone we meet, the Greeks would say, "Grace!" when greeting one another.

The word "grace" is the Greek word *charis*, which means *grace* but also carries the idea of *favor*. So when a person greeted someone with this salutation, it was the same as saying, "I greet you with grace and favor."

But Paul wasn't only addressing the Greek world. As a Jew, he also desired to greet the Jewish world that would be reading his letters. When the Jews met each other, their customary way of greeting one another was to say, "Shalom!"(or "Peace!"). In fact, this is still the customary greeting exchanged between Jews in Israel today.

By using both *grace* and *peace* at the start of his letters, Paul brilliantly reached out and embraced both the Greek and the Jewish world at the outset of his writings. One scholar has said that by using both terms, the doors were thrown open for the whole world to read his letters. It is obvious that Paul deliberately addressed those letters to both the Gentile and Jewish worlds.[5]

For Paul's greetings of "grace and peace," **check out** Romans 1:7; 1 Corinthians 1:3; 2 Corinthians 1:2; Galatians 1:3; Ephesians 1:2; Philippians 1:2; Colossians 1:2; 1 Thessalonians 1:1; 2 Thessalonians 1:2; and Philemon 1:3.

"Grace is not just God's favor that cannot be earned; it is His empowering presence that gives us the ability to live like Jesus. Grace gives us the ability to exceed our own ability! It gives us the ability to live extraordinarily! God didn't just rescue us, but He empowered us so that we can live successfully here in this world."

JOHN BEVERE
adapted from chapter 6

10. According to 1 John 2:6, "Whoever claims to live in him must walk as Jesus did" (NIV). Indeed, as followers of Christ we are to "...walk *worthy of God*" (1 Thessalonians 2:12 NKJV). What is the good news about this command, as well as every other command God gives us in the New Testament?

_____

_____

_____

_____

_____

_____

11. It is very important to remember that grace not only saves us, but it also gives us the ability to live our Christian life the way God has called us to live—*extraordinarily*.

a. Before this session, what was your understanding of God's grace?

_____

_____

_____

b. How has this study, including the analogy of Island Man, reshaped your view?

_____

_____

_____

the bottom line

You have what it takes to please God. He, Himself, gave you the power to do so, and that power is His *grace*. In addition to being God's unmerited favor, grace is also God's power to live like Jesus. Without truly understanding the multifaceted gift of *grace*, you can never function to your full potential and live the extraordinary life God has planned.

FOR FURTHER STUDY

KNOWING THAT YOU ARE SAVED
  Acts 16:31
  Romans 8:16; 10:9-10
  Titus 2:11-12
  1 John 2:3-6; 4:7-8,13-15

GRACE
  2 Corinthians 9:8
  2 Timothy 2:1
  Titus 2:11; 3:7
  Revelation 22:21

GOD'S MERCY
  Psalm 51:1-2
  Proverbs 16:6
  Lamentations 3:22-23
  Titus 3:5

UNVEIL YOUR HERO

...sold his Volkswagen to build 50 circuit boards

Steve Jobs–Founder and CEO of Apple

Journal Your Journey

> ...**Grace** and peace to you many times over as you
> deepen in your experience with God and Jesus, our Master.
> *Everything* that goes into a life of *pleasing God* has been
> miraculously given to us by getting to know, personally
> and intimately, the One who invited us to God.
> The best invitation we ever received!
> —2 Peter 1:2-3 The Message

EYE-OPENERS

Prayerfully, you are learning many new things as you explore the empowering grace of God. What new, eye-opening revelation(s) of truth has the Holy Spirit made real to you in this session?

_____

_____

_____

_____

_____

_____

REVOLUTIONARY YOU

Through your new understanding of God's grace, what is He challenging you to change in your life? How is He asking you to go up higher in your way of living?

_____

_____

_____

_____
_____
_____
_____

PRAYER

*Father, thank You for the awesome gift of Your grace—grace not only to save me and keep me saved but also to **empower** me to live like Christ. I ask You to give me a greater revelation of what Your grace is. Flood my entire being with the power of Your grace—grace to think like Jesus, believe like Jesus, talk like Jesus, and act like Jesus every day and in every way...in Jesus' name, Amen.*

GRACE
IS Power!

> But He gives us more and more grace (**power of the Holy Spirit**, to meet this evil tendency and all others fully). That is why He says, God sets Himself against the proud and haughty, but gives grace [continually] to the lowly (those who are humble enough to receive it).
> —James 4:6 AMP

God's grace is awesome! It is an intangible gift that cannot be earned or bought but can only be received by faith in the one who gives it. God willingly and lovingly chose to save you—forgiving you of your sins and transferring you from the kingdom of darkness into the kingdom of light. This divine favor from our great Creator is definitely unmerited (undeserved and unwarranted).

However, the meaning of God's grace goes far beyond salvation. Grace is His *power*, the supernatural *strength* of His Holy Spirit living in us, transforming us into the very image of Christ. To better understand, read this excerpt on grace and the new birth from **John Wesley**, one of the men of God who helped usher in America's First Great Awakening in the 1700s:

> The born-again person feels in his heart the mighty working of the Spirit of God. This feeling is not in the carnal sense, as the men of the world mistakenly understand the expression, although they have been told again and again its meaning. The meaning is only this, he feels or is inwardly aware of the *graces* which the Spirit of God works in his heart. He feels and is con-

scious of a *peace* which passes all understanding. He many times feels a *joy* in God that is inexpressible and full of glory. He feels the *love* of God shed abroad in his heart by the Holy Spirit which has been given to him. All of his spiritual senses are used to discern spiritual good and evil. He is increasing daily in his knowledge of God and understanding about the inward Kingdom of heaven.

...God continually *breathes*, in a manner of speaking, upon his soul. His soul is continually breathing to God. **Grace** is descending into his heart. His prayer and praise ascends to heaven. By this conversation between God and man, a life of spiritual respiration is set up. Through this, the life of God in the soul is sustained, and this fellowship with the Father and the Son grows. In this manner, the child of God grows up until he comes to full measure of stature in Christ. It clearly appears what the new birth is. Its nature is the great change which God works in the soul when He brings it to life.

...No matter how much a man has attained, or in what high degree he is perfect, he still needs to **grow in grace**. He needs a daily advancement in the knowledge and love of God, his Savior.[6]

Heaven's APPEAL

But **grow in grace** (undeserved favor, spiritual strength) and recognition and knowledge and understanding of our Lord and Savior Jesus Christ (the Messiah). To Him [be] glory (honor, majesty, and splendor) both now and to the day of eternity. Amen (so be it)!
—2 Peter 3:18 AMP

What role does grace play from the time you receive salvation until you stand before God?

_____

_____

_____

_____

_____

_____

_____

_____

_____

_____

_____

_____

_____

_____

_____

GRACE

As mentioned previously, the word *grace* is derived from the Greek word **charis**, which in a general sense means "favor, benefit, or graciousness of manner." It also carries with it the meaning of a "divine influence (*power*) upon the human heart, and its reflection (*manifestation or mirror image*) in a person's life."[7] Grace is a dynamic force that does more than just affect our standing with God by crediting us with righteousness; grace affects our experience as well. It is marked always by God's enabling work within us to overcome our helplessness.[8]

[words in parentheses are synonyms added for clarity and understanding]

God's grace is also often described as His *anointing, strength* and *power*. It is the supernatural ability of His Spirit that makes the seemingly impossible things possible. Looking back over your life, can you recall a time when you sensed God's grace, His holy ease, reflected in your life? Share your experience and what God's grace gave you the power to accomplish.

_____

_____

_____

_____

_____

_____

_____

_____

_____

_____

_____

Meditate on the message of James 4:6 (see page 39) and 1 Peter 5:5. What is the one thing that will cause God to cut off His power supply of grace to you? What attitude must you maintain?

_____

_____

_____

_____

_____

_____

_____

Paul acknowledged that it was only by God's grace that he was able to do *anything*, and the same is true for us. Read 1 Corinthians 15:10 and write what it speaks to your heart.

_____

_____

_____

_____

_____

_____

_____

Also **check out** 1 Corinthians 3:10.

How do you receive grace? Simply by asking! Read Hebrews 4:16 and write what you can do to put into practice this powerful truth.

_____

_____

_____

_____

_____

_____

_____

_____

_____

_____

1. Quotes on *Salvation* (retrieved 3-19-09, www.dailychristianquote.com). 2. Raymond McHenry, *McHenry's Quips, Quotes & Other Notes* (Peabody, MA: Hendrickson Publishers, Inc. 1998) p. 220. 3. Quotes by *Kathryn Kuhlman* (retrieved 3-20-09, www.kathrynkuhlman.com/godsgrace.html). 4. Adapted from *The Word In Life*™ *Study Bible*, Copyright © 1993, 1996 by Thomas Nelson, Inc. Used by permission, p. 337. 5. Rick Renner, *Sparkling Gems from the Greek* (Tulsa, OK: Teach All Nations, 2003) Adapted from p. 848. 6. John Wesley, *The Holy Spirit & Power* (Gainesville, FL: Bridge Logos, 2003) pp. 66, 174. 7. Adapted from *Strong's Exhaustive Concordance of the Bible*, James Strong, LL.D., S.T.D. (Nashville, TN: Thomas Nelson, Inc. 1990). 8. John Bevere, *Extraordinary* (Colorado Springs, CO; WaterBrook Press, 2009) p. 54.

NOTES

For out of His fullness (abundance) we have all received [all had a share and we were all supplied with] one *grace* after another and *spiritual blessing* upon spiritual blessing and even favor upon favor and gift [heaped] upon gift.

For while the Law was given through Moses, **grace** (unearned, undeserved favor and spiritual blessing) and **truth** came through Jesus Christ.

—John 1:16-17 AMP

traordin

Newness of Life 4

Please refer to chapters 7 and 8 in the *Extraordinary* book, along with session 4 of the teaching series.

> The Apostle John writes, 'And of His fullness we have all received, and grace for grace' (John 1:16). Here is the point so many miss today due to incomplete teaching: John connects receiving the *fullness of God's nature* with *grace*. Grace is God's unmerited gift that not only saved us from eternal damnation, but also gave us His characteristics. One aspect of grace is just as real as the other, and it was all provided the moment we were saved.
>
> **JOHN BEVERE**
> adapted from chapter 7

1. As a believer in Jesus Christ, you have been given **newness of life**! First John 4:17 says, "...as He is, so are we in this world," and John 1:16 declares that "...of His fullness we have all received, and grace for grace." In your own words, explain how these two verses are connected and what they say about you as a born-again child of God.

    _____

    _____

    _____

    _____

    _____

    _____

    _____

    _____

2. How you see yourself greatly shapes and influences what you believe and how you act. God wants you to see yourself through *His eyes*, not your own or anyone else's.

a. How do you see yourself—as a *sinner* saved by grace, or a *son* or *daughter* of the Most High who is forgiven by grace and made a part of God's family? What do you think has contributed to your current mindset?

_____

_____

_____

b. *Meditate on the message* of these verses and write what the Lord shows you about who you are in Him.

...God sent forth His Son, born of a woman, born under the law, to redeem those who were under the law, that we might receive the adoption as sons. And because you are sons, God has sent forth the Spirit of His Son into your hearts, crying out, "Abba, Father!" Therefore you are no longer a slave but a son, and if a son, then an heir of God through Christ.
   —Galatians 4:4-7 NKJV

How great is the love the Father has lavished on us, that we should be called children of God! And that is what we are! The reason the world does not know us is that it did not know him. Dear friends, now we are children of God...
   —1 John 3:1-2 NIV

Voice
of the Ages

"We're held back by traditional teaching and 'churchianity.' In the denomination I was raised in, we were famous for saying, 'I'm so weak and unworthy.' We thought we were being humble—we didn't know we were being ignorant! ...
We'd say, 'I'll never amount to anything. I'm just a worm of the dust. Poor ol' me; I'm just a sinner saved by grace.' That's wrong! I'm saved by grace, and I *was* a sinner, but I'm no longer a sinner—now I'm a saint! Sometimes you hear Christians say, 'I'm going to be a saint.' If you're born again, you *are* one already."
   —Kenneth E. Hagin[1]

_____

_____

_____

_____

_____

_____

_____

_____

Check out John 1:12-13.

3. Because grace has been misunderstood and not taught clearly, many Christians today view it as "the Big Cover-Up," but this is completely contrary to what the New Testament teaches.

   a. Explain what is meant when grace is treated as "the Big Cover-Up." (See page 64 in the book.)

   _____

   _____

   _____

   _____

   b. Have you ever used God's grace in this way? What is this called in 2 Corinthians 6:1?

   _____

   _____

   _____

   _____

   _____

4. Since God is *all-knowing*, He knew that mankind would not be able to follow or keep the Law—the Ten Commandments. So, He gave us the Law so we would realize our desperate need for a Savior. (See Romans 3:20 and Galatians 3:19-25.)

   a. Did Jesus come to *get rid of* the Law? Read Matthew 5:17-18 and write His reason for coming.

   _____

   _____

   _____

   _____

   _____

   b. What has been your understanding of grace up until this point?

   _____

   _____

   _____

   _____

   _____

5. In Matthew 5:17-48, Jesus gives six comparisons between life under the Law that came through Moses and new life under grace and truth that came through Him. Read each scripture and explain how Jesus adjusted the Law under grace.

Scriptures	Life under the Law says...	How is this different under grace?
Matthew 5:21-24	Do not murder.	
Matthew 5:27-28	Do not commit adultery.	
Matthew 5:31-32	Divorce permitted with a certificate.	
Matthew 5:33-37	Do not swear falsely; faithfully fulfill your vows.	
Matthew 5:38-42	Revenge permitted; an eye for an eye and a tooth for a tooth.	
Matthew 5:43-47	Love your neighbor and hate your enemies.	

Which would you say is a more strict code to live by: life under the *Law* or life under *truth and grace* brought by Jesus? Why?

_____

_____

_____

_____

How does your answer differ from what you have previously believed and been taught?

_____

_____

_____

_____

> "Because grace came, because God's divine nature was freely imparted to us, because hardened hearts were replaced by the Seed of God's inherent characteristics, we now have the ability to live as He intended mankind to live from the beginning—*extraordinarily*. We now can live this life as *sons and daughters* of God, in His image, His likeness, possessing His ability through grace!"

adapted from chapter 7

Heaven's APPEAL

I'll give you a new heart. I'll put a new spirit in you. I'll cut out your stone heart and replace it with a red-blooded, firm-muscled heart. Then you'll obey my statutes and be careful to obey my commands. You'll be my people! I'll be your God!
—Ezekiel 11:19-20 The Message

6. In the Old Testament, when people repented they wore sackcloth and put ashes on their head to outwardly display an attitude of sincere humility and sorrow for their sin. But as a New Testament believer under grace, repentance is different.

a. In your own words, describe what *true repentance* means and what it involves.

_____

_____

_____

_____

_____

_____

_____

b. According to Proverbs 28:13, what is needed to obtain mercy and break free from sin's grip?

_____

_____

_____

c. Do you find it difficult to confess your sins to God and/or someone close to you? Why or why not?

_____

_____

_____

d. There are two types of sorrow we can experience—*godly* sorrow or *ungodly* sorrow. Read 2 Corinthians 7:9-10 and explain the difference between the two, showing how repentance is related to each.

_____

_____

_____

Voice of the Ages

"*True repentance* will entirely change you; the bias of your souls will be changed, then you will delight in God, in Christ, in His Law, and in His people."
—**George Whitefield**[2]

BAPTIZE

The word *baptize* comes from the Greek word **baptidzo**, which generally means "to dip repeatedly, to immerse, submerge or overwhelm." It also carries with it the idea of *washing* or *making clean*.[3] *Baptidzo* originally meant "to dip and dye," describing the process of dipping a garment into a vat of dye and leaving it there long enough for the material to soak up the new color. When the garment was pulled up out of the dye, its outward appearance was permanently changed. As believers, we are baptized, or submerged, into the blood of Jesus; symbolically, we die with Him and are "dyed" in Him, and our lives are *permanently changed*![4]

7. According to God's Word, once you repent of your sins and invite Jesus into your heart, you are *baptized* into Him and you become a child of God. Through Christ, you are *free from the power of sin* and no longer have a sin nature—you have God's nature.

a. In your own words, explain what it means to be *baptized* into Christ Jesus and into His death.

_____

_____

_____

Check out Romans 6:2-8; 1 Peter 2:24; Galatians 2:20-21.

b. Do you fully believe that you are free from a sin nature? Whether yes or no, what fruit from your life proves this?

_____

_____

_____

c. According to Romans 6:11-14, how does God desire you to *see yourself* in relation to sin, and what does He require you to do to resist the temptation to give in to it?

_____

_____

_____

_____

If possible, **check out** these verses in the Amplified Bible.

d. How are you currently seeing yourself? What do you think has contributed to this view, or mindset?

_____

_____

_____

_____

_____

Heaven's APPEAL

For *your* sake He made Christ [virtually] to be sin Who knew no sin, so that in and through Him *you* might become [endued with, viewed as being in, and example of] the righteousness of God [what *you* ought to be, approved and acceptable and in right relationship with Him, by His goodness].
—2 Corinthians 5:21 AMP
[italicized words personalized for emphasis]

Voice of the Ages

"Learn to know Christ and Him crucified. Learn to sing to Him, and say, 'Lord Jesus, *You are my righteousness*, I am Your sin. You have taken upon Yourself what is mine and given me what is Yours. You have become what You were not so that I might become what I was not.'"
—**Martin Luther**[5]

8. Although grace and mercy are closely related and work hand in hand, they are different. Briefly describe a memorable situation in which God gave you grace and a situation in which He gave you mercy. Tell why you are grateful and express it to the Lord.

God gave me **grace** when...

_____

_____

_____

God gave me **mercy** when...

_____

_____

_____

> **Grace** is when we _get_ what we don't deserve, and **mercy** is when we _don't get_ what we do deserve. Mercy manifests when we don't get justice for our sin. Grace, on the other hand, is imparted power we don't deserve that frees us from the tyranny of sin.

JOHN BEVERE
adapted from chapter 8

9. It is so vital to realize that **words are seeds**, and the type of seed we plant determines the harvest we reap. The words we hear will either empower or disempower us, and the most valuable "seed" we can plant in the soil of our spirit and soul is the _Word of God_.

a. If a person continually hears teaching declaring he/she is just a sinner saved by grace and no different than the world, how will it affect his/her life?

_____

_____

_____

b. If a person continually hears teaching declaring he/she has received the fullness of Christ's nature, how will it affect his/her life?

_____

_____

_____

c. Which teaching have you been more familiar with up until now? How has it affected you?

_____

_____

_____

10. Being ignorant of the truth of God's Word can produce devastating effects in our lives. It can bring us into captivity and ultimately destroy us (see Isaiah 5:13 and Hosea 4:6).

a. What did the Bereans do that made them strong, wise believers? What can you learn from their example and apply in your life?

_____

_____

_____

_____

_____

_____

_____

_____

Check out Acts 17:11.

> *Every* Scripture is **God-breathed** (given by His inspiration) and profitable for instruction, for reproof and conviction of sin, for correction of error and discipline in obedience, [and] for training in righteousness (in holy living, in conformity to God's will in thought, purpose, and action), so that the man of God may be complete and proficient, well fitted and thoroughly equipped for every good work.
> —2 Timothy 3:16-17 **AMP**

Heaven's APPEAL

11. Indeed, the Word of God is amazing! It is the indestructible, incorruptible seed that packs the power to totally transform a person's life. Luke 1:37 says, "...no word from God shall be without power or impossible of fulfillment" (AMP). What God has spoken to us is filled with power and destined to be fulfilled.

Heaven's APPEAL

> *Study* to shew thyself approved unto God, a workman that needeth not to be ashamed, *rightly dividing the word of truth.*
> —2 Timothy 2:15 **KJV**

a. As mighty as the Word of God is, its power can be negated. Explain how it is often *nullified* in your life and the lives of others.

_____

_____

_____

Check out Mark 7:6-13.

b. List some practical things you can do when listening to teaching or reading a book that will help prevent the power of God's Word from being nullified.

_____

_____

_____

_____

c. *Get quiet before the Lord* and take an inventory of the things you believe. What beliefs are you living your life by that are not based on God's Word but on the traditions and opinions of men? Ask the Lord to show you; write what He reveals.

_____

_____

_____

_____

PRAYER OF REPENTANCE

Father, expose the corruptible seeds that have been sown in my heart—those teachings that are contrary to Your Word. I surrender these false beliefs to You; please forgive me for holding onto them or exalting them above the truth of Your Word. From this day forward, open my eyes and ears to the full knowledge of Your Word...reveal to me what it means to be in Christ and all that is mine as a result; help me fully grasp the reality that Your full nature has been deposited in me. Help me to be perfect, growing into the complete, mature image of Jesus...in Jesus' name, Amen.

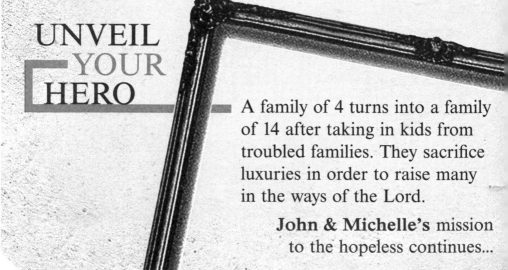

UNVEIL YOUR HERO

A family of 4 turns into a family of 14 after taking in kids from troubled families. They sacrifice luxuries in order to raise many in the ways of the Lord.

John & Michelle's mission to the hopeless continues...

Journal
Your Journey

> Under grace, we now have the nature of Jesus Christ and are able to *live in truth* at all times. We now have *integrity* inbred in our very being. We are now capable of being men and women who are like God, able to say what we mean, mean what we say, and abide by the integrity of our word; for our hearts have been made new and clean by the incorruptible seed of His nature.
>
> **JOHN BEVERE**
> adapted from chapter 7

EYE-OPENERS

By God's grace, you are now beginning to see things about your relationship with God that you have never seen before. Indeed, we have been given an awesome privilege to be called *sons and daughters* of God. What eye-opening revelation(s) of truth is the Holy Spirit making real to you?

_____

_____

_____

_____

REVOLUTIONARY YOU

With any revelation of truth often comes the need to make adjustments in your life. List any *new goals* or *practices* the Lord is prompting you to establish.

_____

_____

_____

_____

the bottom line

Through faith in Jesus Christ, we are given a powerful privilege to reconnect in relationship with our heavenly Father. The moment we repent of our sin and invite Jesus into our life, the divine Seed containing the fullness of God is planted in our spirit and we have a brand new life. Not only does Jesus bring us life-changing *truth*, but He also provides us with *grace*—the divine ability to live the truth. As we continue in His Word and draw on His grace, this Seed grows and matures, producing the fruit of God's character in our lives.

IMPLANTED
with Divine DNA

> You have been *regenerated* (born again), not from a
> mortal origin (seed, sperm), but from one that is immortal
> by the ever living and lasting Word of God.
> —1 Peter 1:23 AMP

Few things on earth are more mysterious and fascinating than a seed. Seeds are the unformed, yet complete expression of its parents—whether plant or person—containing all of the parents' innate characteristics. Seeds are actually a plant within a shell, made in the image of what formed it.

William Jennings Bryan, the 41st U.S. Secretary of State and strong opponent of Darwinism, said it well when he said:

> "I have observed the power of the watermelon seed. It has the power of drawing from the ground and through itself 200,000 times its weight. When you can tell me how it takes this material and out of it colors an outside surface beyond the imitation of art, and then forms inside of it a white rind and within that again a red heart, thickly inlaid with black seeds, each one of which in turn is capable of drawing through itself 200,000 times its weight—when you can explain to me the mystery of a watermelon, you can ask me to explain the mystery of God."[6]

If you are born again, the divine DNA of Almighty God has been deposited in you! All the genetic qualities of Jesus Christ are living inside of you in *seed form* and were planted there the moment you accepted Him as your Savior and Lord. All that is needed for this divine Seed to grow into full maturity is the proper conditions and spiritual nutrients.

" The Seed that was planted in you, which you were recreated through, is none other than Christ Himself; this Seed is indeed incorruptible.
We are in Christ, He is in us, and we have the fullness of His nature. The Seed planted in us when we were born again is all that makes Christ who He is! How awesome. In this world we have the comprehensiveness of His nature! "

JOHN BEVERE
adapted from chapter 7

Meditate on the message of 1 John 3:9 in these three different versions of the Bible:

> No one born (begotten) of God [deliberately, knowingly, and habitually] practices sin, for **God's nature** abides in him [His principle of life, *the divine sperm*, remains permanently within him]; and he cannot practice sinning because he is born (begotten) of God.
>
> **—Amplifed**

> The person who has been born into God's family does not make a practice of sinning because now **God's life** is in him; so he can't keep on sinning, for this new life has been born into him and controls him—he has been born again.
>
> **—The Living Bible**

> People conceived and brought into life by God don't make a practice of sin. How could they? **God's seed** is deep within them, making them who they are.
>
> **—The Message**

What is the Holy Spirit revealing to you about the Seed of God planted in you?

_____

_____

What is He showing you about sin?

_____

_____

Take a few moments to carefully read through the Fascinating Fact about the *Mystery & Magnificence of a Seed*, then answer the questions.

FASCINATING FACT:
THE MYSTERY & MAGNIFICENCE OF A SEED
What is a SEED? It is the substance that nature prepares for the reproduction, propagation and conservation of the species; that from which anything springs; first principle, original.[7]

Seeds fundamentally are a means of reproduction. A typical seed includes *three* basic parts: (1) an *embryo*, (2) a *supply of nutrients* for the embryo, and (3) a *seed coat*. The embryo is an immature plant from which the new plant will grow under proper conditions. The supply of nutrients within the seed is what the new seedling (embryo) will grow from. The seed coat helps protect the embryo from mechanical injury and from drying out.

In a mature seed, the seed coat can be a paper-thin layer, like a peanut, or something more substantial, like the thick and hard seed coat of a coconut.[8]

A seed *germinates*, or sprouts, usually after a period of dormancy. Over time, the seed absorbs water, warms and cools, takes in available oxygen, and soaks up sunlight. Eventually, all these factors work to initiate the germination process. When the temperature is suitable and there is an adequate supply of moisture, oxygen and light, the seed absorbs water and swells, rupturing the seed coat. The growing tip of the undeveloped root emerges first, followed by the growing tip of the emergent shoot. The seed's supply of nutrients provides energy for the early stages of this process, until the seedling is able to manufacture its own food via photosynthesis.[9]

Just as natural seeds need regular watering, adequate sunlight and good soil, the divine Seed of God in you needs specific spiritual nutrients to germinate and grow. Check out these scriptures to determine some of the nutrients you need for the Seed of God to grow in you. From each group, write out the verse that touches your heart most.

WATER – Psalm 1:2-3; 119:103 • Ephesians 5:26 • 1 Peter 2:2 • Joshua 1:8

_____

_____

LIGHT – John 8:12 • Psalm 16:11 • Hebrews 1:3 • 1 John 1:7

_____

_____

SOIL – Proverbs 27:17 • Ecclesiastes 4:9-10 • Hebrews 10:25

_____

_____

TEMPERATURE – James 1:2-3,12 • 1 Peter 1:6-7; 4:12-13 • 2 Peter 2:9 • Revelation 2:10

_____

_____

FOR FURTHER STUDY

YOU ARE DEAD TO SIN
    Romans 6:2,11
    Galatians 5:24
    Colossians 3:3
    1 Peter 2:24

CHRIST IS THE WORD
    John 1:1,14
    1 John 1:1-3
    Revelation 19:13

NOTES

1. Kenneth E. Hagin, *Zoe: The God-Kind of Life* (Tulsa, OK: Kenneth Hagin Ministries, 2006) p. 58. 2. Quotes on *Repentance* (www.dailychristianquote.com, retrieved 4-4-09). 3. Adapted from *Thayer's Greek-English Lexicon of the New Testament*, Joseph H. Thayer (Grand Rapids, MI: Baker Book House Company, 1977) p. 94. 4. Rick Renner, *Sparkling Gems from the Greek* (Tulsa, OK: Teach All Nations, 2003); adapted from p. 330. 5. Quotes by *Martin Luther*, see note 2. 6. Illustrations on the *God, Nature Of* (www.sermonillustrations.com, retrieved 4-8-09). 7. Adapted from *Noah Webster's First Edition of an American Dictionary of the English Language* (1828), Republished in facsimile edition by Foundation for American Christian Education (San Francisco, CA 1995). 8. Adapted from the definition of *Seeds* (www.answers.com/topic/seed#Seed_functions, retrieved 4-8-09). 9. Ibid.

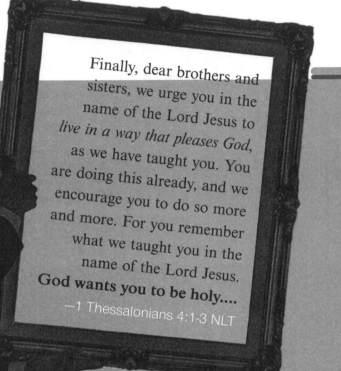

Finally, dear brothers and sisters, we urge you in the name of the Lord Jesus to *live in a way that pleases God,* as we have taught you. You are doing this already, and we encourage you to do so more and more. For you remember what we taught you in the name of the Lord Jesus. **God wants you to be holy....**

—1 Thessalonians 4:1-3 NLT

xtraordin

Holiness 5

Please refer to chapters 9 and 10 in the *Extraordinary* book, along with session 5 of the teaching series.

HOLINESS

The word *holiness*, from the Greek word *hagiasmos*, signifies separation—separated *from* sin and consecrated *to* God. It is the resulting state of conduct that fits those who are separated unto God. Holiness is often translated as, and synonymous with, the word *sanctification*, the state pre-determined by God for believers, into which He calls them, and in which they begin their Christian course and so pursue it. Becoming a sanctified one, or saint, is *not* an attainment; it is a condition or position into which God in *grace* calls men.[1] This pure, sinless, upright state is maintained under the influence or power of the Holy Spirit.[2]

Heaven's APPEAL

But now since you have been set free from sin and have become the slaves of God, you have your *present reward* in **holiness** and its end is eternal life.

—Romans 6:22 AMP

1. One of the greatest rewards of living life empowered by God's grace is *holiness*—the divine ability to live separated from the sinful ways of the world and set apart for His service. (See Ephesians 5:1.)

   a. How are you to *receive* and *cooperate with* God's grace daily in order to live a holy life? (See page 85 in the book.)

   _____

   _____

   _____

   _____

   _____

Check out Proverbs 3:5-7; Hebrews 4:16; James 4:6.

> ❝*True holiness* is very appealing and important. Jesus is not coming back for a contaminated, worldly church but a church 'not having spot or wrinkle or any such thing.' The church will be 'holy and without blemish' (Ephesians 5:27). So since it's a holy church Jesus will be coming back for, we definitely want to know all about holiness.❞
>
> **JOHN BEVERE**
> adapted from chapter 9

2. Holiness is not about rules and regulations that focus on meaningless *outer* restrictions. True holiness is a genuine transformation—it's living on a level of extraordinary excellence in purity and separation that is evident in all you do.

    a. In the book, John states two reasons he believes holiness has not been discussed much in churches today (see pages 84-85). What are those reasons? How are you challenged by them?

    _____

    _____

    _____

    b. Being set apart—holiness—does not mean you are to live totally separated from non-Christians. How can you engage the lost—let your light shine before all—and remain pure? What does this look like for you on a practical level?

    _____

    _____

    _____

    _____

    _____

    _____

    _____

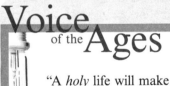

Voice of the Ages

"A *holy* life will make the deepest impression. Lighthouses blow no horns, they just shine."
—D. L. Moody[3]

Check out John 17:15-20; 1 Corinthians 5:9-11.

> ❝When God says, 'Be holy as I am holy,' He is actually saying, 'I don't think, talk or live like you, so come up to My level of living.' To put it in more blunt language, He's saying, 'Why do you want to hang around the barnyard and live like turkeys when I've called you to soar like eagles! I've called you to an *extraordinary* life!'❞
>
> **JOHN BEVERE**
> adapted from chapter 9

3. To understand holiness is to understand sanctification. In your own words, briefly explain sanctification and how it differs from *justification*. What does each involve, when do they take place, and what part does God play and what part do you play?

JUSTIFICATION (salvation from eternal death)

_____

_____

_____

_____

_____

SANCTIFICATION (holiness)

_____

_____

_____

_____

Check out pages 91-92 in the book for help.

4. Do you truly desire *holiness*? How important is *purity* to you? Here are some candid questions to help you see deeper into your heart:

LOCATE YOUR HEART. ASK YOURSELF...

What kind of things do I *talk about* most of the time?

_____

_____

_____

What kind of things do I often *pray about*?

_____

_____

_____

What kind of things do I regularly *spend money* on?

_____

_____

_____

What kind of things do I frequently *give my time and attention* to?

_____

_____

_____

Overall, *what or whom am I living for?*

_____

_____

_____

Now, stop and review your answers. To a great degree, these are the things that are driving your life. Do you see a pattern? What would you say is motivating your life most? Is the Holy Spirit prompting you to make any changes? If so, what are they?

_____

_____

_____

5. It pleases God when we live holy—especially in our sexuality. Read the strong warning against sexual immorality and rebellion in 1 Corinthians 10:1-12. Pay close attention to the miracles the Lord manifested, the attitudes and actions of the Israelites, and the consequences that resulted.

a. How does this passage of Scripture speak to you personally? What parallels, if any, do you see between the lives of the Israelites and your life?

_____

_____

_____

_____

_____

Heaven's APPEAL

If then you have been raised with Christ [to a new life, thus sharing His resurrection from the dead], aim at and seek the [rich, eternal treasures] that are above, where Christ is, seated at the right hand of God. And *set your minds* and *keep them set* on **what is above** (the higher things), not on the things that are on the earth. For [as far as this world is concerned] you have died, and your [new, real] life is hidden with Christ in God.
—Colossians 3:1-3 AMP

b. Is the Holy Spirit showing you anything you need to repent of? If so, take a moment to pray; write down anything He reveals.

_____

_____

_____

_____

Voice of the Ages

"It is written of our blessed Lord, 'Thou hast loved righteousness, and hated iniquity; therefore God, even thy God, hath anointed thee with the oil of gladness above thy fellows.' It is the purpose of God that we, as we are indwelt by the Spirit of His Son, should likewise *love righteousness* and *hate iniquity*. ...I believe that, as we are filled with the desire to press on into this life of *true holiness*, desiring only the glory of God, there is nothing that can hinder our true advancement."

—Smith Wigglesworth[4]

6. There are a number of believers who struggle with fornication, adultery, pornography, masturbation, homosexuality or other forms of sexual impurity. Usually the struggle to get to a place of true freedom results from a more deeply rooted problem, such as pride, rebellion, or unforgiveness. Whatever the issue, the root is always *a lack of the true fear of the Lord*. (See page 86 in the book.)

a. Are you struggling with sexual sin? *Get quiet before the Lord* and ask Him to show you anything in your heart that may be hindering you from experiencing the full freedom Jesus died to give you.

_____

_____

_____

_____

_____

_____

_____

_____

_____

Check out Romans 12:1; Galatians 5:16; Colossians 3:5-6.

BREAK FREE FROM HABITUAL SIN!

Breaking free from repetitive, habitual sin *is* possible by God's grace. However, it's often a process that takes time. We don't get into a pattern of wrong behavior overnight, and we don't get out of it overnight.

ADMIT you have a problem. Call sin, sin; agree with God that it's wrong, and repent.

SUBMIT yourself to God. *Humble yourself* and receive His inexhaustible grace continually.

COMMIT yourself to the Word. Saturate yourself in *specific scriptures* that counter the conduct you want to be free from.

PRAY & SAY the Word over your life and against the enemy as needed throughout the day.

ANSWER to someone trustworthy. Be *accountable* to someone who loves you enough not to condone your sin or condemn you when you fall, someone who will confront you in love.

These suggested steps are meant merely to be a guideline to victory. They will help produce the character of Christ in your life as you *starve your flesh* and *feed your spirit*. **Check out** *Living a Pure Life* on workbook page 73.

7. Living together, having sex outside of marriage, and getting divorced and remarried for reasons *other than* unfaithfulness have become more and more common among professing Christians. Why is this the case? What do you think is needed to see this trend reversed? (See page 88 in the book.)

_____

_____

_____

_____

8. Seeing people *participate* in immoral behavior hurts the heart of God greatly. But according to Scripture, something else is equally offensive. What is it and what are the consequences? (See page 86 in the book.)

_____

_____

_____

_____

_____

Check out 1 Samuel 3:10-14; Romans 1:28-32; 1 Corinthians 5.

a. How does this challenge you?

_____

_____

_____

9. According to 2 Corinthians 7:1, we are to "...cleanse ourselves from **everything** that *contaminates* and *defiles* body and spirit, and bring [our] consecration to completeness in the [reverential] fear of God" (AMP).

For question "a," **check out** Galatians 5:19-21; 2 Timothy 3:2-5 and pages 91-92 in the book.

a. List some things that contaminate us *inwardly* and *outwardly* that we must cleanse ourselves of. Jot down any contaminants you are dealing with personally.

INWARDLY

_____

_____

_____

_____

OUTWARDLY

_____

_____

_____

_____

I AM PERSONALLY DEALING WITH...

_____

_____

_____

Voice of the Ages

"By *sanctification* the Son of God is formed in me, then I have to transform my natural life into a spiritual life by *obedience* to Him. God educates us down to the scruple. When He begins to check, do not confer with flesh and blood, *cleanse yourself* at once. Keep yourself cleansed in your daily walk... I have the responsibility of keeping my spirit in agreement with His Spirit, and *by degrees* Jesus lifts me up to where He lived—in perfect consecration to His Father's will, paying no attention to any other thing. Am I perfecting this type of *holiness* in the fear of God? Is God getting His way with me, and are other people beginning to see God in my life more and more?"

—**Oswald Chambers**[5]

b. How do we cleanse ourselves of impurities? Read the verses below, and in your own words explain what this means.

Isaiah 1:16-20 • Ephesians 4:22-24 • James 4:7-10

_____

_____

_____

_____

_____

_____

Heaven's APPEAL

...For as you yielded your bodily members [and faculties] as servants to impurity and ever increasing lawlessness, so now **yield** your bodily members [and faculties] once for all as servants *to righteousness* (right being and doing) [which leads] to sanctification.

—Romans 6:19 AMP

FASCINATING FACT: CLEAN HANDS

Hospital-acquired infections are one of the leading causes of death in the United States. These infections are either the direct or indirect cause of 80,000 fatalities a year. As many as one-third of these deaths could be prevented if health care workers strictly followed infection control procedures. Of those precautionary measures, "hand washing may be the single most important tool of infection prevention." Studies suggest that health care workers wash their hands less than half as often as they should. "Patients come into the hospitals to be made better, and they actually, in many cases, are made worse," said Dr. Robert Haley, director of epidemiology at the University of Texas Southwestern Medical School in Dallas. These hospital infections cost the hospitals between $4 and $4.5 billion a year.

The church has frequently been compared to a hospital. *Do we compare here*? People are looking for a safe haven to find God, but sometimes our churches send them home with a greater illness. This could be prevented if we would but heed the words of James 4:8, "Draw near to God and He will draw near to you. *Cleanse your hands*, you sinners; and *purify your hearts*, you double-minded." Daily hand washing at the basin of God's Word will prevent us from spreading the deadly germs of sin.[6]

10. In the story of "Island Man," we find that after he was given the gun, symbolizing the empowering gift of God's grace, he failed to put it to use. As a result of *wasting* the resources he was given, he *fell short* of the goal of freedom and eventually died.

a. In what ways can you personally identify with Island Man?

_____

_____

_____

b. According to 2 Peter 2:20-22 and Hebrews 12:14-15, what are the tragic results of falling short of God's grace—failing to cooperate with His power and walk in holiness?

_____

_____

_____

_____

_____

_____

_____

Voice of the Ages

"The instrument through which you see God is your *whole self*. And if a man's self is not kept *clean* and *bright*, his glimpse of God will be blurred— like the Moon seen through a dirty telescope."

—**C. S. Lewis**[7]

"If we're not walking in holiness, we don't have the ability to behold God in our hearts. Therefore, we are not being changed (2 Corinthians 3:18). We're getting *information* but not *transformation*. And that is a recipe for becoming religious."

JOHN BEVERE
adapted from chapter 9

11. Read Isaiah 35:8-10 on the following page that describes the *Highway of Holiness*.

a. What kind of people and things will you find on this road? Who will you *not* find?

_____

_____

b. How does the Highway of Holiness compare with the Narrow Road Jesus talks about in Matthew 7:13-14?

_____

_____

_____

There will be a highway there, called '*The Road of Holiness*.' No sinner will ever travel that road; no fools will mislead those who follow it. No lions will be there; no fierce animals will pass that way. Those whom the Lord has rescued will travel home by that road. They will reach Jerusalem (heaven) with gladness, singing and shouting for joy. They will be happy forever, forever free from sorrow and grief.

—Isaiah 35:8-10 TEV

[word in parentheses added for emphasis]

12. We are living in the last days. In 2 Timothy 3:1 TLB, Paul said, "In the last days it is going to be very difficult to be a Christian."

a. Why is this and how does it relate to God's grace?

_____
_____
_____
_____
_____
_____
_____
_____
_____
_____
_____
_____

Check out 2 Timothy 3:2-5.

" God says, when we walk in the power of the grace of God, bearing true fruits of holiness, *we are invincible because of Him*. ...We are invincible, not because of our own ability, but because of the ability grace provides. So, in essence, **grace gives us the power** to walk the highway of holiness, which secures us the promise of finishing the race well. It keeps us from becoming shipwrecked in our faith and falling short. "

JOHN BEVERE
adapted from chapter 10

b. What makes this condition so dangerous to others and the cause of Christ? (See pages 102-103 in the book.)

_____
_____
_____
_____
_____
_____

c. Read 1 Corinthians 5:9-13; 15:33 and 2 Thessalonians 3:6 regarding the company you keep. Write what the scriptures speak to your heart and any changes the Lord is prompting you to make in this area.

_____

_____

_____

_____

d. What can you do, or are you currently doing, to ensure that you are living righteously and above reproach?

_____

_____

_____

_____

the bottom line

God desires and requires us to be holy, just as He is holy. Holiness means to live as Jesus and be pure in every area of your life, including sexuality. The great news is that He has given us power to do so in the form of His *grace*. As we cooperate with the Holy Spirit and the grace He supplies, we can live an extraordinary life of holiness in the midst of a dark and perverse generation.

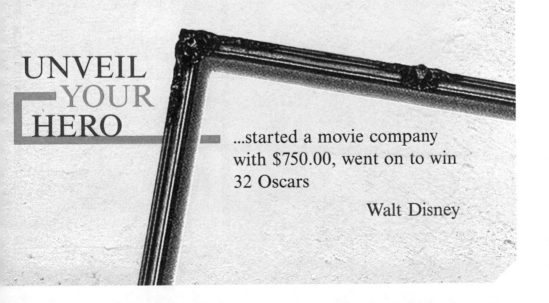

UNVEIL YOUR HERO

...started a movie company with $750.00, went on to win 32 Oscars

Walt Disney

Journal
Your Journey

" My friend, don't fight for 'your right' to habitually live in sin and still make it to heaven. That is the wrong way of viewing life.
Rather, realize God has given you an amazing gift—freedom!
You don't have to sin any longer; what you couldn't free yourself from before, you now can live free from through the power of His amazing grace! "

JOHN BEVERE
adapted from chapter 10

EYE-OPENERS

Understanding what true holiness is and its inseparable connection to the empowering grace of God is vital to pleasing Him. Take a moment and write down some of the eye-opening principles the Holy Spirit is showing you.

_____

_____

_____

_____

REVOLUTIONARY YOU

More than likely, you've been challenged by this session. What changes do you sense the Lord is motivating you to make to better reflect His holy nature? Is He asking you to set any *new goals*?

_____

_____

_____

_____

_____

_____

_____

_____

_____

_____

_____

Heaven's
APPEAL

So think clearly and exercise self-control. Look forward to the special blessings that will come to you at the return of Jesus Christ. Obey God because you are his children. Don't slip back into your old ways of doing evil; you didn't know any better then. But now **you must be holy in everything you do,** just as God—who chose you to be his children—is holy. For he himself has said, 'You must be holy because I am holy.'

—1 Peter 1:13-16 NLT

Living a PURE Life

How can a young person stay pure? By obeying your word and following its rules.
—Psalm 119:9 NLT

PURE

Clear; free from mixture; free from moral defilement; without spot; not sullied or tarnished; incorrupt, genuine, real, true, unadulterated, unpolluted, clean; separate from any other substance or from everything foreign; *holy*.[8]

I think most would agree...we live in a sex-saturated society that seems to sink deeper into impurity with each passing day. Lewd language and obscene images permeate media of all kinds, not to mention the pornography industry, which pulls in an estimated $12-13 billion a year.[9] In such a cesspool of sin surrounding us on all sides, *how are we to keep ourselves pure*? It all starts with God's Word.

Feeding your spirit a steady, well-balanced diet of God's Word will provide you with health in every area of your life. And while you *feed your spirit*, you must also *starve your flesh*. What you starve will grow weak, and what you feed will grow strong. This is the repeated principle of Galatians 5:16, Colossians 3:5, 1 Peter 2:11 and many other verses of Scripture. **Billy Graham** echoes this truth with eloquence in his book *The Secret of Happiness*:

> All transgression begins with sinful thinking. You who have come to Christ for a *pure heart*, **guard** against the pictures of lewdness and sensuality which Satan flashes upon the screen of your imaginations, select with care the *books* you read, choose discerningly the kind of *entertainment* you attend, the kind of *associates* with whom you mingle, and the kind of *environment* in which you place yourself. You should no more allow sinful imaginations to accumulate in your mind and soul than you would let garbage collect in your living room.[10]

As you starve your five senses of impure things and feed your spirit the pure milk and meat of the Word, your life will become purer. God's Word in the hands of His Holy Spirit and empowered by His grace is invincible!

GUARD YOUR **HEART** AND **EYES**

Remember, Jesus said to *look* upon a woman lustfully is to commit adultery (see Matthew 5:28). "Your *eyes* are the lamp for your body. When your eyes are good, you have all the light you need. But when your eyes are bad, everything is dark" (Luke 11:34 CEV). *Meditate on the message* and **hide in your heart** these powerful words of wisdom:

Heaven's APPEAL

Pure and undefiled religion before God and the Father is this: to visit (care for and help) orphans and widows in their trouble, and to **keep oneself unspotted (uncontaminated, unpolluted) from the world.**
—James 1:27 NKJV
[words in parentheses added for clarity]

Above all else, guard your *heart*, for it affects everything you do. Avoid all perverse talk; stay far from corrupt speech. Look straight ahead, and *fix your eyes* on what lies before you. (NLT)

Above all else, guard your *affections*. For they influence everything else in your life. Spurn the careless kiss of a prostitute. Stay far from her. *Look straight ahead*; don't even turn your head to look. (TLB)
—Proverbs 4:23-25

I made a covenant with my *eyes* not to look lustfully at a girl. (NIV)
I made a solemn pact with myself never to undress a girl with my *eyes*. (THE MESSAGE)
—Job 31:1

Let your way in life be far from her (lust, impurity), and come not near the door of her house [*avoid the very scenes of temptation*].
—Proverbs 5:8 AMP
[words in parentheses added for clarity]

What do these verses speak to you about guarding yourself from the impurities that you deal with every day? *Get quiet before the Lord* and ask Him to give you a practical plan of action to **avoid the very scenes of temptation** at work, at home, on the Internet, etc.

_____

_____

_____

_____

_____

_____

_____

_____

_____

_____

_____

INVENTORY YOUR LIFE

Is there anything in your life that is feeding your flesh—impurities you're trying to break free from? If so, it's time to get rid of them and replace them with pure alternatives. The same holds true for the people you're keeping company with. Ask the Lord for His input in these areas.

THE THINGS IN MY LIFE THAT NEED TO CHANGE ARE...

_____

_____

_____

_____

_____

What are some of the benefits of living a PURE life? **Check out** Psalm 24:3-6 and Matthew 5:8 for some inspiring insights.

_____

_____

_____

_____

_____

_____

_____

_____

_____

Heaven's APPEAL

> But solid food is for full-grown men, for those whose **senses and mental faculties are** *trained by practice* to discriminate and distinguish between what is morally good and noble and what is evil and contrary either to divine or human law.
>
> —Hebrews 5:14 AMP

As you continue to feed on the meat of God's Word, the way you *think*, *talk*, and *act* is revolutionized. Over time, your "...*senses* and *mental faculties* are **trained by practice** to discriminate and distinguish between what is morally good and noble and what is evil and contrary either to divine or human law." As John so effectively expressed, "Our flesh can *be trained in righteousness*, and it loves habitual patterns." Therefore, we must train it with Truth!

Get quiet before the Lord. Ask Him to give you a creative and effective plan of action to *read, study, meditate on* and *speak* the Word over your life. Write what He reveals and ask Him for the grace to discipline your flesh to carry it out.

_____

_____

_____

_____

Once you are set free from the deadly grip of sexual impurity or any form of sin, you must *continue* to resist the desire to accept the thoughts and engage in the actions that once enslaved you; you must learn to *cooperate with God's grace* given to you by the Holy Spirit. Ultimately, as you abide in the Word and in prayer, God will change your desires!

FOR FURTHER STUDY

PURITY OF GOD'S WORD
Psalm 12:6; 19:8; 119:40
Proverbs 30:5
John 15:3; 17:17
Ephesians 5:26-27

KEEPING A PURE MIND
Psalm 1:1-3; 51:10-12
Proverbs 15:26
Romans 12:2
Ephesians 4:22-24

THE EFFECTS OF RELATIONSHIPS
Proverbs 13:20
1 Corinthians 15:33
2 Thessalonians 3:14
Ephesians 5:3-7

1. Adapted from *Vine's Complete Expository Dictionary of Old and New Testament Words*, W. E. Vine (Nashville, TN: Thomas Nelson, Inc. 1996) pp. 307-308. 2. *Thayer's Greek-English Lexicon of the New Testament*, Joseph H. Thayer (Grand Rapids, MI: Baker Book House Company, 1977) p. 7. 3. Quotes on *Holy* (www.sermonillustrations.com/a-z/holy.htm, retrieved 4/16/09). 4. *Standing Firm, 365 Devotions to Strengthen Your Faith*, compiled by Patti M. Hummel (St. San Luis Obispo, CA: Parable) p. 206. 5. Oswald Chambers, *My Utmost for His Highest* (Uhrichsville, OH: Barbour Publishing, Inc., MCMXCVII) p. 78. 6. Raymond McHenry, *McHenry's Quips, Quotes & Other Notes* (Peabody, MA: Hendrickson Publishers, Inc. 1998) p. 46. 7. C.S. Lewis, *The Quotable Lewis* (Carol Stream, IL: Tyndale House Publishers, Inc. 1990) p. 504. 8. *Noah Webster's First Edition of an American Dictionary of the English Language* (1828), Republished in facsimile edition by Foundation for American Christian Education (San Francisco, CA 1995). 9. Laurie Hall, *An Affair of the Mind* (Wheaton, IL: Tyndale House Publishers, 2003) p. 11. 10. Billy Graham, *The Secret of Happiness* (Garden City, NY: Doubleday & Company, Inc., 1955) pp. 79-80.

NOTES

...The Kingdom of God isn't ushered in with visible signs. You won't be able to say, "It has begun here in this place or there in that part of the country." For the Kingdom of God is **within you.**

—Luke 17:20-21 TLB

The Kingdom Within

Please refer to chapter 11 in the *Extraordinary* book, along with session 6 of the teaching series.

THE KINGDOM OF GOD

The *Kingdom of God* is the sphere of God's rule (see Psalm 22:28; 145:13). Since, however, this earth is presently in universal rebellion against God, the "kingdom" of God is the sphere in which, at any given time, *His rule is acknowledged*. God calls upon men and women everywhere, without distinction of race or nationality, to submit voluntarily to His rule. Thus the "kingdom" is said to be "in mystery" now (see Mark 4:11). As a result, at the present time and so far as this earth is concerned, **the Kingdom of God is** *where the King is* and *where His rule is acknowledged*—first, in the heart of the individual believer and then in the churches of God.[1]

> "Once the Holy Spirit came to dwell *within* mankind, the Kingdom and all its power would be **within us**! We now possess the power to advance the Kingdom in the hearts and lives of others. This is why God's Word states, 'For God's Kingdom is not a matter of eating and drinking, but of the righteousness, peace, and joy which the Holy Spirit gives' (Romans 14:17 TEV)."
>
> **JOHN BEVERE**
> adapted from chapter 11

1. Jesus is the head of His church—the growing body of believers He ransomed and rescued from Satan's rule. Although Jesus is no longer physically here on earth, we are, and He deeply desires to continue manifesting the lasting fruit of His Kingdom through us.

   a. Explain the difference between the Kingdom of God being *near*, or at hand, and it being *here*.

The Kingdom being NEAR (at hand) means...

_____

_____

Check out Matthew 3:1-2; 10:5-8; Mark 1:14-15.

79

The Kingdom being HERE means...

Check out John 14:16-17; Acts 2:1-4; 1 Corinthians 3:16.

b. How are you praying for *God's Kingdom to come* in your life, your family, your church, your neighborhood, your country, etc.? What fruit of these prayers are you seeing?

Heaven's APPEAL

...When you pray, say: Our Father in heaven, hallowed be Your name. **Your Kingdom come.** *Your will be done on earth as it is in heaven.*
—Luke 11:2 NKJV

2. When Jesus sent out the disciples to declare and demonstrate God's Kingdom *on earth as it is in heaven*, the disciples looked for certain conditions in the lives of the people—conditions that were contrary to the conditions of heaven.

a. In what specific ways did Jesus and His disciples visibly manifest the Kingdom of God in the lives of people on the earth?

Check out Matthew 10:1,7-8; 11:4-5; 15:29-37.

b. What conditions are in your life and the lives of those around you that are *contrary* to the conditions of heaven? What is the Lord stirring in your heart to do about it?

APPEAL

In solemn truth I tell you, *anyone believing in me* shall do the same miracles I have done, and **even greater ones**, because I am going to be with the Father. You can ask him for *anything*, using my name, and I will do it, for this will bring praise to the Father because of what I, the Son, will do for you. Yes, ask *anything*, using my name, and I will do it!

—John 14:12-14 TLB

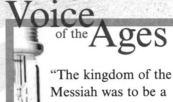

Voice of the Ages

"The kingdom of the Messiah was to be a **spiritual kingdom**, not temporal. It has a spiritual influence. The Kingdom of God will not change men's outward condition, but their *hearts* and *lives*. Therefore, look for the Kingdom of God in the revolutions of the heart, not of the civil government."

—**Matthew Henry**[2]

3. The Pharisees had *great expectations*; they believed the Messiah was coming but that He would come a certain way—as a conquering king, not a suffering one. Their inability or unwillingness to be flexible in their faith created an impenetrable prison that barred them from God's presence.

a. Have you ever prayed for Jesus to come and help you, and He showed up in an *unexpected* way? Explain the situation and how you had to adjust your expectations.

_____

_____

_____

_____

b. *Get quiet before the Lord* and ask Him what (if any) "prisons" are barring you from experiencing His presence on a deeper and more intimate level.

_____

_____

_____

_____

_____

RIGHTEOUSNESS

The word *righteousness* is the Greek word *dikaiosune*. It is used in one form or another about 228 times in the New Testament and at least 40 times in the book of Romans. The word *righteous* goes back to a base word, *reg*, which means to "move in a straight line." Thus, *righteous* (rightwise) means "in the straight (or right) way." When used to reference morality, *righteous* means "living or acting in the right way." What's the "right" way? Scripture gives us the ultimate standard of rightness or *righteousness*—it is **God Himself**. God's character reveals what is absolutely right. Not only is He the measure of moral right and wrong, He's also the *source* of right living.[3] To be righteous is to be *right in the eyes of God*.

4. One of the most important aspects of the Kingdom of God that Jesus brought to earth is righteousness. The Word is full of scriptures describing the *righteousness* of God and His Son Jesus.

a. *Meditate on the message* of these scriptures:

> But seek (aim at and strive after) **first of all** His *Kingdom* and His *righteousness* (His way of doing and being right), and then all these things taken together will be given you besides.
> —**Matthew 6:33 AMP**

> For the *Kingdom of God* is not eating and drinking, but **righteousness** and peace and joy in the Holy Spirit.
> —**Romans 14:17 NKJV**

> For the *Kingdom of God* is not just fancy talk; it is living by God's power.
>
> —**1 Corinthians 4:20 NLT**

b. Read Galatians 3:6-9, describing how Abraham was counted as righteous in God's sight. What does this say to you about being counted as righteous in His sight?

_____

_____

_____

Also **check out** Romans 4:18-22; James 2:23; 2 Corinthians 5:21.

FASCINATING FACT:
THE DUAL DUTY OF GOD'S SPIRIT

Jesus' personal ministry on earth was *limited* to the individuals with whom He came into contact with in His physical body. The Holy Spirit, however, is not limited by the restrictions of a physical body. Jesus sent the Holy Spirit not only to be our Comforter, but also to go into all the world and work through redeemed beings as agents to manifest God's Kingdom on earth as it is in heaven.

The Holy Spirit works in all people to guide them into all truth.[4]

For more on the **ministry of the Holy Spirit**, see John 14:15-20,26; 16:5-15.

5. After Jesus was raised from the dead, He walked the earth for 40 days, appearing to hundreds of His followers. Before He returned to heaven, He told them to wait for the promise of the Father—that He Himself would send the *Holy Spirit*.

    a. What were the disciples filled with power to do—and what are *you* filled with power to do? (See page 111 in the book.)

    _____

    _____

    _____

    b. The Holy Spirit was not just given to the disciples, the early church, and certain "full-Gospel, charismatic" believers; He was given to *everyone*. What does the timeless truth in Acts 2:39 speak to your heart?

    _____

    _____

    _____

> "Not only was great grace upon the apostles to advance the Kingdom, but also on the ordinary church members. This was God's will *then*, this is God's will *now*, and this will *always* be God's will!"
>
> **JOHN BEVERE**
> adapted from chapter 11

Heaven's APPEAL

...with **great power** the apostles gave witness to the resurrection of the Lord Jesus. And **great grace** was upon them all.
—Acts 4:33 NKJV

6. To a great degree in the western Church, the miraculous is missing—the "greater works" that Jesus declared we would do aren't being done. Read the stories of Peter and John at the temple in Acts 3:1-10 and 4:1-4.

EXTRAORDINARY DEVOTIONAL WORKBOOK

a. How did the people in the temple respond to Peter and John—the *messengers* of the Gospel? How did they respond to the *message* of the Gospel?

_____

_____

_____

_____

_____

_____

_____

_____

b. How do you think the people would have responded if Peter and John would have just gone into the temple and preached *without* bringing healing to the crippled man?

_____

_____

_____

_____

_____

_____

Voice of the Ages

"...There is no greater power in the world than the power of the Holy Spirit. ...[Jesus] promised, 'And ye shall receive **power**' (Acts 1:8). In other words, Jesus was saying, 'I give you the *same power* that was manifested in My life on earth, the *same power* that was manifested in My ministry. You have seen the miracles. You have seen the demonstration of supernatural power. Now I am going away, but I am not leaving you powerless. As a gift, I am giving to you, My own church, the *same power* that was Mine when I walked this earth.'"

—**Kathryn Kuhlman**[5]

c. **Check out** the mighty miracles done through Peter (Acts 9:32-35), Paul (Acts 16:25-34), and Jesus (John 4:46-53). After reading these accounts of the manifestation of God's Kingdom, write what the Holy Spirit reveals to you about why we desperately need miracles in the church today.

_____

_____

_____

_____

Heaven's APPEAL

Jesus said, "Don't believe me **unless I do miracles** of God. But if I do, believe them even if you don't believe me. Then you will become convinced that the Father is in me, and I in the Father."

—John 10:37-38 TLB

MANIFEST

The word *manifest* means "to reveal, to display, or to make appear; to show plainly; to make public; to reveal to the eye or to the understanding." A *manifestation* is "the act of making known what is secret, unseen or obscure; the display of anything by clear evidence."[6] Therefore, the manifestations of God are the bringing out into the open public the excellent character and conduct of God.

7. Jesus Christ effectively brought heaven to earth, Himself being an exact representation of the Father. He said, "...He who has seen Me has seen the Father..." (John 14:9). In the same way, Jesus sends us into the world to represent Him (see John 20:21).

a. When was the last time you personally experienced the Kingdom of God manifested before your eyes? Explain what took place and how it changed your life.

_____

_____

_____

_____

_____

_____

_____

_____

_____

_____

_____

b. Jesus' mission is now YOUR mission! Read His declaration in Luke 4:18-19 and write what it means to you personally.

_____

_____

_____

_____

66 Jesus makes it crystal clear: He tells us once that *the Kingdom is within us*. We can advance it, no matter if we are a businessman or woman, stay-at-home mom, doctor, school teacher, mechanic, student, politician, investor, realtor—our occupation does not matter. He commissions **all of us** to advance the Kingdom. 99

JOHN BEVERE
adapted from chapter 11

Heaven's APPEAL

He said to them, "Go throughout the whole world and preach the gospel to all people. Whoever believes and is baptized will be saved; whoever does not believe will be condemned. **Believers will be given the power to perform miracles**: they will drive out demons in my name; they will speak in strange tongues; if they pick up snakes or drink any poison, they will not be harmed; they will place their hands on sick people, and these will get well."

—Mark 16:15-18 TEV

8. Part of advancing God's Kingdom is proclaiming the Gospel and seeing people saved. In the first five chapters of the book of Acts, it repeatedly says that souls were *added* to the church. But after chapter five, the Word says that the number of disciples *multiplied* greatly.

a. What took place that caused the growth to change from addition to multiplication?

_____

_____

_____

_____

_____

_____

_____

b. What does this say to you about reaching the lost of this generation with the saving message of Christ?

_____

_____

Check out Acts 2:41,47; 5:14 for verses on addition; Acts 6:1,7 for verses on multiplication.

c. Is there anything holding you back from using God's grace to manifest His Kingdom on earth? Are you afraid of something? *Get quiet before the Lord* and ask Him to show you your heart; write what He reveals and surrender any fears or hindrances to Him in prayer.

Heaven's APPEAL

I sought the Lord, and he answered me; *he delivered me from all my fears.*

—Psalm 34:4 NIV

_____

_____

_____

_____

_____

_____

_____

_____

9. Stephen was *not* an apostle, prophet, teacher or pastor. He was a "restaurant" worker who helped with the distribution of food for widows. And yet, the Word says he was full of God's *grace* and *power*, performing amazing miracles among the people.

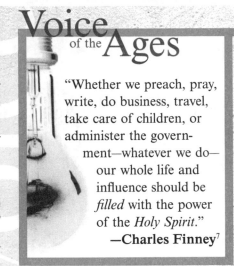

Voice of the Ages

"Whether we preach, pray, write, do business, travel, take care of children, or administer the government—whatever we do—our whole life and influence should be *filled* with the power of the *Holy Spirit*."
—**Charles Finney**[7]

   a. How does the life of Stephen, an ordinary believer living an extraordinary life, challenge you?

   _____

   _____

   _____

   _____

   b. Do you ever become fearful about what you'll say as a witness for Christ when you stand before others? Write, in your own words, God's encouraging promise in Luke 12:11-12.

   _____

   _____

   _____

10. Like Jesus, Stephen had the grace to forgive his murderers. Is there someone who has really hurt you who has been hard to forgive? God's grace is available to empower you to freely forgive him/her. Humble yourself before God in prayer and ask Him for help. Write out anything He reveals to you about the situation.

   _____

   _____

   _____

   _____

the bottom line

Grace is God's empowerment; it is the expression of His Kingdom that now dwells *within* you as a believer. Grace gives you the ability to go beyond your own ability in every area of life—to live like Jesus and do what is needed to advance His Kingdom. This extraordinary living pleases Him greatly!

UNVEIL YOUR HERO

A former prisoner—completely transformed—returns to his old neighborhood to do youth ministry and use his story to reach those he used to "run" with.

Myron is shaping a generation...

Journal Your Journey

"**The Kingdom within** speaks of the divine nature, which empowers us to live holy and fruitful in this present world. Jesus showed how mankind was created to live, not bound to the burning desires of fallen flesh, but motivated by righteousness, propelled by the power of the Holy Spirit in love, joy, and peace—abounding in forgiveness, healing, restoration, and lifting others to the higher life. *This is the Kingdom*; it's not only to live holy, but also to bring heaven's lifestyle to our lost and dying world."

JOHN BEVERE
adapted from chapter 11

EYE-OPENERS
What new, eye-opening understanding(s) about the Kingdom of God is the Holy Spirit bringing to life in your heart?

_____

_____

_____

_____

REVOLUTIONARY YOU
How is your faith being stretched? How is the Lord challenging you to change your thinking? What *new goals* is He asking you to set?

_____

_____

_____

PRAYER

Father, thank You for a greater understanding of Your Kingdom within me. I pray that Your Kingdom would come and Your will would be done through me on earth as it is in heaven. Please stir up in me an appetite for the extraordinary. Give me a hunger and thirst for righteousness so that I may be filled with all that You are (Matthew 5:6)...in Jesus' name, Amen.

EVERYTHING!

For in Christ there is all of God in a human body;
so **you have everything** when you have Christ,
and *you are filled with God* through your union with Christ.
He is the highest Ruler, with authority over every other power.
—Colossians 2:9-10 TLB

A cataclysmic event took place 50 days after Jesus was raised from the dead—an event without equal in history before or since. It was the day of Pentecost—the day that unleashed a brand new paradigm of God's power in the earth. On that day, **everything** that Jesus paid for was made available and *deposited within* believers—*everything*.

For the first time, the Spirit of the Living God was poured out not just *on* people, but *in* people. And unlike the Old Testament times when God's Spirit came on certain people for a certain task, this time His Spirit was *permanently* poured into people from all walks of life (see 1 John 2:27). Imagine! The same Spirit that raised Christ from the dead, created the heavens and the earth, and formed the complex anatomy of every living creature we see could now make His home *inside* of believers of every language in every land!

FASCINATING FACT: EXPLOSIVE & SUSTAINING POWER

Power can be *unleashed*, or it can be *harnessed*. The energy in 10 gallons of gasoline, for instance, can be released explosively by dropping a lighted match into the can. Or it can be channeled through the engine of a car in a controlled burn and used to transport a person 350 miles.

Explosions are spectacular, but controlled burns have *lasting effect*, staying power. The Holy Spirit works **both** ways. At Pentecost, He exploded on the scene; His presence was like "tongues of fire" (Acts 2:3). Thousands were affected by one burst of God's power. But He also works through the church—the body of Christ—where God released the Holy Spirit's power for the long haul.[8]

It is very important to understand that the infilling of God's Spirit that took place on the day of Pentecost is *different* from the initial indwelling of God's Spirit that we receive when we get saved. The same day Jesus was raised from the dead, He appeared to His disciples and "...He breathed on them, and said to them, 'Receive the Holy Spirit'" (John 20:22). Then 40 days later, the day He ascended into heaven, He "...commanded them not to depart from Jerusalem, but to wait for the Promise of the Father, ...for John truly baptized with water, but you shall be baptized with the Holy Spirit not many days from now" (Acts 1:4-5).

Why would Jesus breathe on His disciples to receive the Holy Spirit one day, and then 40 days later command them to wait in Jerusalem for the baptism of the Holy Spirit if these two experiences were not different? It is the baptism of the Holy Spirit that empowers us with His abounding grace to be His witnesses. This immersion in God's power will give you **everything** you need to live holy and advance His Kingdom on every level.

Abounding, empowering grace gives us complete and total sufficiency to meet **every** need we may encounter, no matter what it is! There is nothing that cannot be accomplished in regard to bringing heaven's provision—*God's Kingdom*—to earth; for grace has fully provided it all!

JOHN BEVERE
adapted from chapter 11

Heaven's APPEAL

And God is able to make **all grace** (every favor and earthly blessing) come to you *in abundance*, so that you may always and under all circumstances and whatever the need be self-sufficient [possessing enough to require no aid or support and furnished in abundance for every good work and charitable donation].
—2 Corinthians 9:8 AMP

Read Acts 1:8 and explain why you too need God's promised gift of the Holy Spirit.

_____
_____
_____
_____
_____
_____
_____

How did the baptism of the Holy Spirit affect the disciples? Look at a *before* and *after* snapshot.

BEFORE the day of Pentecost, the disciples were...

_____

_____

Check out Matthew 26:56; Mark 14:50; John 20:19.

AFTER the day of Pentecost, the disciples were...

_____

_____

Check out Acts 4:5-13; 23-33.

Check out Jude 20, Romans 8:26-27 and 1 Corinthians 14:2,4 to understand some of the priceless blessings of praying in the Spirit. Write what the Spirit reveals to you.

_____

_____

_____

If you have received the baptism of the Holy Spirit, are you speaking in tongues regularly? If not, why?

_____

_____

_____

If you have received Jesus as your Lord and Savior but have not received the promised gift of the Holy Spirit, you can do so now. All you have to do is ask! Jesus said, "If you then, though you are evil (*have a fallen nature*), know how to give good gifts to your children, how much more will your Father in heaven give the Holy Spirit to those who ask him!" (Luke 11:13 NIV; italic words added for clarity). Just believe in your heart that what you ask for is given to you the moment you ask (see James 1:6-7; Mark 11:24).

Once you *ask* for the Holy Spirit, you will *receive* the Holy Spirit. Acts 2:4 says, "And they were all filled with the

Heaven's APPEAL

May blessing...be to the God and Father of our Lord Jesus Christ (the Messiah) Who has blessed us in Christ with **every** spiritual (given by the Holy Spirit) blessing in the heavenly realm!

—Ephesians 1:3 AMP

Holy Spirit and began to speak with other tongues, as the Spirit gave them utterance." The word *utterance* means "syllables, sounds or words." After you pray, you will probably sense a syllable, sound or word bubbling up inside of your spirit or swirling around in your head. Although the impression may be faint and you may feel silly, SPEAK IT OUT! That's the Holy Spirit. He is giving you the utterance, but you must YIELD your lips, tongue and vocal chords to speak what He is impressing on you.

Are you ready to receive? Do you believe you will have what you ask for? Are you willing to yield yourself to the Holy Spirit? Let's pray...

Prayer for the Promised Gift of the Holy Spirit
Father, I come to You in the name of Jesus. First, I ask You to forgive me of any sin, including the sin of unforgiveness, that would hinder me from receiving from You. By Your grace and as an act of my will, I release anyone who has offended me and bless them with Your best; wash me clean from the inside out with the blood of Jesus.

Now as Your child, I ask You for the promised gift of the Holy Spirit. You said if I ask You for the Holy Spirit, You would give Him to me, so by faith I ask You now to baptize me with Your Holy Spirit. I receive everything You have for me, including the ability to speak in a new heavenly language. Now in faith, I will speak in new tongues...in Jesus' name, Amen!

Has the Lord touched your life? Take a few moments to express your experience.

_____

_____

_____

FOR FURTHER STUDY

RIGHTEOUSNESS
  Isaiah 61:10
  Romans 10:4
  1 Corinthians 1:30
  Philippians 3:9

MINISTRY OF THE HOLY SPIRIT
  John 6:63; 14:15-26; 16:7-15
  Romans 8:11
  2 Corinthians 3:6
  1 John 2:27

BAPTISM OF THE HOLY SPIRIT
  Joel 2:28-29
  Matthew 3:11
  John 7:38-39
  Acts 1:4-5,8; 2:1-21,38-39

NOTES

1. Adapted from *Vine's Complete Expository Dictionary of Old and New Testament Words*, W. E. Vine (Nashville, TN: Thomas Nelson, Inc. 1996) p. 344. 2. *The KJV Matthew Henry Study Bible*, Kenneth Abraham, General Editor (Word Bible Publishers, Inc.: 1994) p. 2020. 3. From *The Word in Life*™ Study Bible, copyright © 1993, 1996 by Thomas Nelson, Inc. Used by permission, adapted from p. 2025. 4. Ralph M. Riggs, *The Life of Christ* (Springfield, MO: Gospel Publishing House, 1968) adapted from p. 186. 5. Kathryn Kuhlman, *The Greatest Power in the World* (North Brunswick, NJ: Bridge-Logos Publishers, 1997) pp. 65-66. 6. Adapted from *Noah Webster's First Edition of an American Dictionary of the English Language* (1828), Republished in facsimile edition by Foundation for American Christian Education (San Francisco, CA 1995). 7. *Fast Break, Five-Minute Devotions to Start Your Day* (St. San Luis Obispo, CA: Parable, 2007) p. 117. 8. Illustrations on *Pentecost* (www.sermonillustrations.com/a-z/p/pentecost.htm, retrieved 4/23/09).

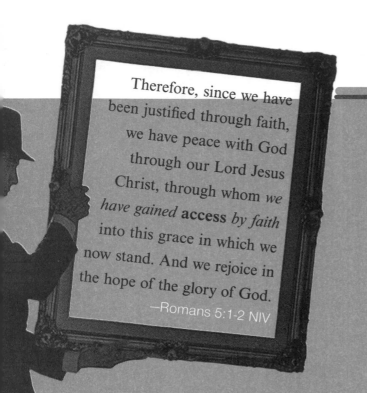

Therefore, since we have been justified through faith, we have peace with God through our Lord Jesus Christ, through whom *we have gained* **access** *by faith* into this grace in which we now stand. And we rejoice in the hope of the glory of God.

—Romans 5:1-2 NIV

xtraordin

The Access

7

Please refer to chapter 12 in the *Extraordinary* book, along with session 7 of the teaching series.

ACCESS

The capacity to enter or approach; a way of approach. To *access* something means to "get at or gain entrance."[1] Synonyms for *access* include: the right to use, the way in, to get into, or admittance.

> Simply put, faith is the 'pipeline' of grace. Hear Paul's words once again— 'we have *access* by faith into this grace wherein we stand.' Faith is the determining factor of whether we *do* or *do not* partake of grace. This means the grace—the empowerment needed to please God—that we've carefully discussed in all our previous sessions cannot be accessed any other way than through faith!
>
> **JOHN BEVERE**
> adapted from chapter 12

1. Our **faith** is like a "PVC pipeline" that taps into and brings us the "water supply" of God's grace. Consequently, it's important that you keep your pipeline of faith connected to the Source and clear of all debris.

   a. Hebrews 11:6 gives us two indispensable ingredients to having faith. In your own words, describe what those are.

   _____

   _____

   b. What kind of things tend to "clog" your pipeline of faith, causing the flow of God's grace in your life to be cut off?

   _____

   _____

   Get quiet before the Lord and ask Him for His insight in this area of your life. Surrender any hindrances to Him in prayer and ask Him for wisdom and grace to overcome these obstacles.

95

Voice of the Ages

"**Faith** occupies the position of a *channel* or *conduit pipe*. **Grace** is the *fountain* and the *stream*. Faith is the aqueduct along which the flood of mercy flows down to refresh the thirsty sons of men. ...The aqueduct must be kept intact to carry the current. Similarly, faith must be true and sound. It must lead right up to God and come right down to ourselves so that it may become a serviceable channel of mercy to our souls."

—**Charles H. Spurgeon**[2]

2. Everything you need to live extraordinarily is contained within God's Word—the word of His grace. *Meditate on the message* of the scriptures below:

Therefore they stayed there a long time, speaking boldly in the Lord, who was bearing witness to **the word of His grace**, granting signs and wonders to be done by their hands.

—Acts 14:3

So now, brethren, I commend you to God and to **the word of His grace**, which is *able to build you up* and give you an inheritance among all those who are sanctified.

—Acts 20:32

(Jesus) being the brightness of His glory and the express image of His person, and upholding all things by **the word of His power**...

—Hebrews 1:3

[word in parentheses added for clarity]

a. What does the phrase "word of His grace/power" communicate? How is it activated?

_____

_____

_____

b. How would the meaning be different if the verses were written "power of His Word"? (See page 123 in the book.)

_____

_____

_____

_____

"All of God's power is contained in His Word. This is why the enemy has fought to get our churches to preach inspired messages out of newspapers or coaches' manuals instead of the Word of God. ...We've gotten away from the Word; we've wanted to inspire and come up with something new, when in reality God is saying, 'Why are you looking for something new when I have put all of My power within the *Word of My grace?'*"

JOHN BEVERE
adapted from session 7

3. God's Word declares that salvation is available to all through faith in Jesus Christ. Yet, according to Matthew 7:13-14, the majority of mankind is going to end up in hell, eternally separate from God, although this is *not* His will. Read 1 Timothy 2:4 and 2 Peter 3:9 and explain what God's will is concerning the salvation of mankind.

_____

_____

_____

_____

Also **check out** Isaiah 48:9; Romans 9:22; 1 Peter 3:20, declaring God's patience with sinners. Let all these scriptures encourage and motivate you to continue to pray for your lost loved ones. God wants them saved even more than you do!

4. Read Hebrews 3:12-4:12—a passage containing the story of the Israelites and the importance of having a right heart before the Lord.

a. What did the Israelites consistently do that deeply angered God?

_____

_____

_____

_____

b. What did they *fail to do* with the message of Truth they heard that canceled its power? What happened to them as a result? How does this speak to you personally?

_____

_____

_____

_____

5. Have you ever prayed and asked God, "What do I need to do to see Your works take place?" If so, you're not alone; in fact, that's exactly what Jesus' followers asked Him in John 6:28.

    a. Write out John 6:29—Jesus' answer to them, and consequently us, explaining what needs to be done in order to see His miracles manifest.

    _____

    _____

    _____ John 6:29

    Also **check out** John 14:1 and 1 John 3:23.

    b. God can be trusted! Write what these truths declaring His faithfulness to keep His Word speak to your heart:

    Numbers 23:19 • Psalm 18:30 • Matthew 24:35

Heaven's
APPEAL

...**Believe** in the Lord Jesus Christ [*give yourself up to Him, take yourself out of your own keeping and entrust yourself into His keeping*] and you will be saved, [and this applies both to] you and your household as well.
—Acts 16:31 AMP

6. There are many rewards etched in Scripture for those who *believe* and *trust* God—both in this life and the one to come **Check out** these verses and name the *benefits of believing* associated with each:

Scriptures	YOUR BENEFIT FOR *BELIEVING* GOD
Romans 1:16 / 1 John 5:1	
John 5:24; 6:47	
Romans 3:22; 10:4	
1 Peter 2:6 / Isaiah 28:16	
Jeremiah 17:7-8	
Romans 15:13	
John 7:38-39	

John 11:40	
Hebrews 4:3	
1 John 5:5	

Voice of the Ages

THE SOURCE & STRENGTH OF FAITH

"God specifically says that to 'every man that is among you' (every Christian) He has given a starting point in faith. We don't have to generate the first little bit. God gives to each of us a *measure of faith* with which to begin.[3]

...Jesus is the *Author* and *Finisher* of our faith (Hebrews 12:2). He is the beginner and the ender, the *giver* and the *protector* of our faith. ...The essence of it flows out of Him to us. Faith is not generated by man. Faith is not conceived by a preacher, a denomination, or a philosophy. Jesus Christ is the Author of Faith.[4]

...Living faith is obtained individually by individuals from their *living relationship* with *God* and *His Word*. Testimonies related to faith inspire us. But they do not generate that force of power it takes to do the job in our own lives. That comes only out of the Word of God—by reading it, absorbing it, letting it come alive within us.[5]

—Dr. Lester Sumrall

7. Where do you initially *get* faith, the ability to believe? It comes from God Himself (Romans 12:3). How does your faith *grow*? Your "...faith comes by *hearing*, and *hearing* by the word of God" (Romans 10:17).

   a. Explain what the word *hearing* means in both places of this verse and how it is connected with Jesus' words, "He who has ears to hear, let him hear."

   _____

   _____

   _____

   _____

   _____

b. What conditions are needed to be able to *hear* and *receive* the Word of grace?

_____

_____

_____

Check out Matthew 13:23; Luke 8:15; Acts 17:11; 1 Thessalonians 2:13.

Voice of the Ages

"[Abraham] was 'fully assured that what [God] had promised He was able also to perform.' Ah, child of God, for every look at the unlikelihood of the promise, take 10 looks at the promise: this is the way in which faith waxes strong. '*Looking unto the promise of God*, he wavered not through unbelief, but waxed strong' (Romans 4:20, R.V.)."

—**F.B. Meyer**[6]

8. Abraham led an amazing life of faith. He believed God would honor His word and give him a son in his old age, making him the *father of many nations*. Yes, the thought of his age and the barrenness of Sarah's womb did cross his mind, but He did not focus on it. Instead, *he focused on God's promise* to him.

a. Share of a time in your life when God spoke something to you and you had faith in what He said until He made it a reality.

_____

_____

_____

_____

_____

b. How is this experience still affecting your faith today? How about the faith of others?

_____

_____

c. Like Abraham, have you ever experienced a time when God asked you to do something that seemed would cause the *death of the dream* He promised? If so, explain what happened and what you learned from it.

_____

_____

_____

9. One of the greatest *evidences* that we truly have faith in God's Word is found in the *words* we speak—especially when we are under pressure. (See Psalm 116:10, Romans 10:6-8 and 2 Corinthians 4:13.)

   a. What kind of words and phrases often come out of your mouth when times are tough?

   _____
   _____
   _____

Heaven's
APPEAL

...For out of the abundance of the heart the mouth speaks (NKJV). A good man's speech reveals the rich treasures within him. An evil-hearted man is filled with venom, and his speech reveals it (TLB).
                        —Matthew 12:34-35

   b. If your words have sounded more like what *ordinary* men would say under difficult circumstances, it's time to dig deep into God's Word for some *extraordinary* alternatives. Grab a Bible concordance and search for scriptures that address the situations you're struggling with; doing a keyword search may be helpful. Write out the verses that come alive in your heart, and begin to *speak* them aloud over your life and the situations you face. Also, *get quiet before the Lord* and ask Him for a specific word for your current situation.

   _____
   _____
   _____
   _____
   _____
   _____

Use a Strong's Concordance, a concordance in the back of your Bible, or an online search engine like www.biblegateway.com to look up key words for the issues that seem to steal your faith like worry, fear, disappointment, anger, etc.

Heaven's
APPEAL

Now **FAITH** is the assurance (the confirmation, the title deed) of the things [we] hope for, being the proof of things [we] do not see and the conviction of their reality [faith perceiving as real fact what is not revealed to the senses].
                        —Hebrews 11:1 AMP

10. Abraham's trust in God was so great that he was willing to do whatever God told him to do. His corresponding *actions of obedience* were evidence that he truly feared God and **believed His Word** over everything else.

a. What promise has God made to you that you are presently trusting Him to bring to pass?

_____

_____

b. What **words**—especially scriptures—are you speaking aloud that *agree* with the promise?

_____

_____

c. Most often, our job leading up to receiving God's promise is simply to wait and allow Him to bring it to pass. Occasionally He will call us to action and require our obedience. What (if any) **actions** has He prompted you to take? Have you taken them? If not, why?

_____

_____

> **Faith** deeply believes God will do what He says, and it subsequently produces *words of agreement* and *actions of obedience*. ...You can repeatedly declare, 'I'm saved by grace,' boast in God's goodness, speak of love, and use other Christian clichés, but unless there are corresponding actions—*a lifestyle that pleases God*—your faith is empty chatter.
>
> **JOHN BEVERE**
> adapted from chapter 12

Heaven's APPEAL

...Does merely *talking* about faith indicate that a person really has it? ...Isn't it obvious that God-talk without God-acts is outrageous nonsense? ...You can no more show me your works apart from your faith than I can show you my faith apart from my works. Faith and works, works and faith, fit together hand in glove.

—James 2:14,17-18
The Message

11. It's important to understand that true faith always displays itself in *actions*. God's Word says that we are not saved by doing good works; however, if we are saved, *we will do good works* as a result.

a. Explain the difference between not working *for* your salvation and working *because* of your salvation.

Being saved by faith and not by works means...

_____

_____

Check out Ephesians 2:8-9; 2 Timothy 1:9.

Yet, my faith must be backed up by godly actions...

_____

_____

Check out James 2:14-26; Matthew 25:31-46.

b. Read Hebrews 13:16 and 1 John 3:18 and write what they speak to you.

_____

_____

12. Galatians 3:1-14 explains the futility of trying to serve God and become a strong Christian by just following rules. Indeed, anyone who attempts to keep the requirements of the Law but fails in just *one area* is guilty of breaking it all and is under a curse.

a. Trying to live right in your *own ability* is trusting in your flesh. According to John 6:63 and Romans 7:18, how valuable is your flesh?

_____

_____

_____

_____

_____

b. In your own words, write what Galatians 3:11-14 means to you.

_____

_____

_____

_____

_____

Heaven's APPEAL

For we hold that a man is justi-fied and made upright **by faith** *independent of* and distinctly *apart from good deeds* (works of the Law). [The observance of the Law has nothing to do with justification.]
—Romans 3:28 AMP

Voice of the Ages

"Never make a *Christ* out of your faith, nor think of faith as if it were the independent source of your salvation. Our life is found in 'look-ing unto Jesus' (Hebrews 12:2), not in looking to our faith. By faith all things become possible to us. Yet *the power is not in the faith but in the God* in whom faith relies."
—**Charles H. Spurgeon**[7]

UNVEIL YOUR HERO

...dropped out of Harvard to work on a little business idea
Bill Gates–CEO of Microsoft

the bottom line

The awesome gift of God's grace is accessed through our *faith* in Him. Genuine faith is not only heard in our words, but also seen in our actions. As we continue in the Word, our faith grows, God's power is released, and we are able to live a life that pleases Him.

Heaven's APPEAL

But if you are led by the Spirit, you are not under law.
—Galatians 5:18 NIV

Journal Your Journey

Every God-begotten person conquers the world's ways.
The conquering power that brings the world to its knees is our **faith**.
The person who wins out over the world's ways is simply
the one who *believes* Jesus is the Son of God.
—1 John 5:4-5 The Message

EYE-OPENERS

Without doubt, the Holy Spirit has been speaking to you throughout this session. Take a few moments to jot down any eye-opening revelation(s) He's bringing to mind.

_____
_____
_____
_____
_____
_____
_____

REVOLUTIONARY YOU

As the Lord tugs on your heart to climb higher in Him, in what *new ways* is He asking you to look at and operate in faith? Is He prompting you to set any *new goals*? If so, what are they?

_____

_____

_____

_____

_____

Father, thank You for this foundational teaching on faith and grace. Please forgive me for the times when the words of my mouth have been more negative and fear-filled than faith-filled. I ask You to help me reprogram my thinking according to Your ways; as I read and study Your Word, help me find the specific scriptures to speak over my life until they become a part of me. Holy Spirit, show me what corresponding faith-filled actions I need to take and when to take them. I realize that I cannot fulfill Your promised plan for my life in my own ability. I need Your powerful grace, which is only accessed through faith. I believe my faith will grow as I feed on Your Word...in Jesus' name, Amen.

FREE ACCESS

> In [Jesus], *because of our faith in Him*, we dare to have
> the boldness (courage and confidence) of **free access**
> (an unreserved approach to God with freedom and without fear).
> —Ephesians 3:12 AMP
> [word in brackets added for clarity]

Anytime, anywhere, about anything—that is the kind of access you have to Almighty God, the Creator of heaven and earth, through prayer. This free access is not just available to pastors, evangelists, and mighty men and women of state; it is available to *you* as a child of the Most High.

Again, faith is the access to God's grace, or divine power. Consequently, the foremost action demonstrating our faith is prayer. We can and should turn to God anytime, anywhere, about anything and seek His wisdom, direction, and intervention. Prayer should always be our first response, not our last resort. You are not annoying God by your requests; He yearns to be welcomed into every part of your life!

EXTRAORDINARY DEVOTIONAL WORKBOOK

Heaven's APPEAL

...The Spirit Whom He has caused to dwell in us *yearns* over us and He yearns for the Spirit [to be welcome] with a jealous love.

—James 4:5 AMP

How often does God want us to pray? First Thessalonians 5:17 clearly declares His desire: "Pray continually" (NIV). Now, this doesn't mean you have to be on your knees, in your prayer closet or at your church 24/7. Prayer simply means staying connected to God in conversation—*talking with* and *listening to Him* throughout your day.

Jeanne Guyon, a well-known author of the 17th century, has influenced many, including John Wesley, Watchman Nee, and Hudson Taylor. Read this excerpt on "the prayer of simplicity" from her book *Experiencing the Depths of Jesus Christ*:

"Let me ask you, then, do you desire to know the Lord in a deep way? God has made such an experience, such a walk, possible for you. He has made it possible through the **grace** He has given to all His redeemed children. He has done it by the means of His Holy Spirit.

You see, the only way to be perfect is to walk in the presence of God. The only way you can live in His presence in uninterrupted fellowship is by means of **prayer**, but a very special kind of prayer. It is a prayer that leads you into the presence of God and keeps you there at all times; a prayer that can be experienced under any conditions, any place, and any time.

Is there really such a prayer? Does such an experience with Christ truly exist? Yes, there is such a prayer! A prayer that does not interfere with your outward activities or your daily routine.

...May I hasten to say that the kind of prayer I am speaking of is not a prayer that comes from your mind. It is a prayer that begins in the **heart**. It does not come from your understanding or your thoughts. ...Prayer that comes out of the heart is not interrupted by thinking! I will go so far as to say that nothing can interrupt this prayer, *the prayer of simplicity*."[8]

What is the Holy Spirit making alive in your heart through Jeanne Guyon's words?

_____

_____

_____

_____

_____

When anxiety, worry or fear comes against you, the *first* thing to do is pray. Write out these inspiring instructions to help you maintain your faith when trouble comes.

EPHESIANS 6:18

_____
_____
_____
_____
_____
_____

PHILIPPIANS 4:6-7

_____
_____
_____
_____

For the eyes of the Lord are intently watching all who live good lives, and he gives attention when they cry to him. Yes, *the Lord hears the good man* when he calls to him for help, and saves him out of all his troubles.

—Psalm 34:15,17 TLB

The greatest element in *the prayer of simplicity* is God's Word. Isaiah 62:6 says, "...You who [are His servants and by your **prayers**] put the Lord in remembrance [of His promises], keep not silence" (AMP). As we learned earlier, God is not a liar; He keeps His Word. In Jeremiah 1:12, He says, "...I am alert and active, *watching over My word* to perform it" (AMP).

Meditate on the message of these verses and, in your own words, describe the importance and power of continuing in God's Word as it relates to prayer.

PENETRATE

To enter into; to pierce or permeate; to see into or understand; to affect deeply.[9] Words synonymous with *penetrate* include: break through, access, seep or soak into, to infuse.

John 15:7 • 1 John 3:21-24; 5:14-15 • Romans 1:16 • Hebrews 4:12

_____
_____
_____
_____
_____
_____
_____

> ❝Only the **Word of God** has the ability to penetrate right into our heart—it's the only thing that can pass through our conscious mind, intellect or emotions, and reach into our core being where true faith is spawned. Knowing this causes us to realize how important it is to *speak the Word of God*—not to speak tradition, leadership principles, philosophical ideas, concepts of God, and so forth. *Only the Word can penetrate our hearts to produce true faith.*❞
>
> **JOHN BEVERE**
> adapted from session 7 and chapter 12

There are times when we are temporarily denied access. **Check out** these revealing truths and list some of the common conditions that "pull the plug" on your prayers.

Psalm 66:18-20 • Proverbs 28:9 • Isaiah 59:1-2 • Zechariah 7:11-14 • James 4:3

_____

_____

_____

_____

Do you feel like something is hindering your access to the Father's presence? Is the Holy Spirit showing you anything from the scriptures you just read? *Get quiet before the Lord* and bear your heart. Repent of anything you need to, receive His forgiveness, and resume your free access of fellowship with Him!

FOR FURTHER STUDY

ACCESS TO GOD
John 10:9; 14:6
Ephesians 2:18-19
1 Timothy 2:5
Hebrews 10:19-23

GOD KEEPS HIS WORD
Hebrews 6:18; Titus 1:2
Psalm 12:6; Proverbs 30:5
Luke 21:33; 1 Peter 1:25

PRAYER
1 Chronicles 16:11
Psalm 4:3; Proverbs 15:29
Matthew 7:7-11; 26:41; Luke 18:1
Colossians 4:2; James 5:13; Revelation 5:8

NOTES

1. Adapted from *Merriam-Webster's Desk Dictionary* (Springfield, MA: Merriam Webster, Inc. 1995). 2. C.H. Spurgeon, *All of Grace* (New Kensington, PA: Whitaker House, 1981) pp. 56-57. 3. Dr. Lester Sumrall, *Faith Can Change Your World* (South Bend, IN: Sumrall Publishing, 1999) p. 24. 4. Ibid., p. 66. 5. Ibid., p. 13 6. F.B. Meyer, *Abraham: The Obedience of Faith* (Chattanooga,TN: AMG Publishers, 2001) p. 70. 7. See note 2, p. 57. 8. Jeanne Guyon, *Experiencing the Depths of Jesus Christ* (Jacksonville, FL: SeedSowers Publishing, MCMLXXV) pp. 3-4. 9. See note 1.

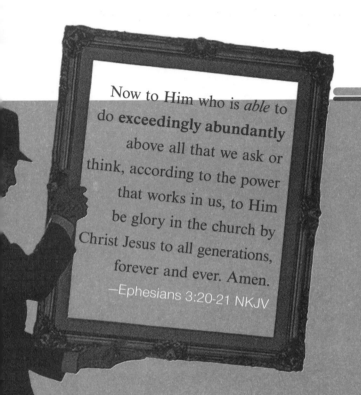

Now to Him who is *able* to do **exceedingly abundantly** above all that we ask or think, according to the power that works in us, to Him be glory in the church by Christ Jesus to all generations, forever and ever. Amen.

—Ephesians 3:20-21 NKJV

xtraordin

Beyond Comprehension

Please refer to chapter 13 in the *Extraordinary* book, along with session 8 of the teaching series.

> "Grace, though it's freely given, can only be accessed through faith, and we tap into its riches through believing. If you can settle this truth in your heart and mind, you'll avoid being misled by *inaccurate feelings*, *contrary circumstances*, or lies of the enemy. ...Our entire walk, from the day we come into God's family until we behold Him face to face, **is all about believing His Word** over what we *see*, *hear*, or *experience*."
>
> **JOHN BEVERE**
> adapted from chapter 13

1. As a believer, your life is founded on faith from start to finish. Indeed, God's Word clearly states that the just and righteous shall live *by faith* (see Hebrews 10:38).

   a. How does your faith help you keep God's commands without becoming burdened by them (see 1 John 5:3-4)?

   _____

   _____

   _____

   _____

Heaven's APPEAL

This Good News tells us how God makes us right in his sight. This is accomplished from start to finish by **faith**. As the Scriptures say, "It is *through faith* that a righteous person has life."

—Romans 1:17 NLT

2. We see in Scripture that as *faith* and *humility* go hand in hand, so do *unbelief* and *pride*. Actually, unbelief is pride and disobedience in disguise—it's what kept the Israelites from entering the Promised Land.

EXTRAORDINARY DEVOTIONAL WORKBOOK

Check out the story of the 12 spies and how God dealt with Israel's unbelief in Numbers 13 and 14.

a. What did the 10 spies who gave a negative report base their calculations of taking the land on? What did Joshua and Caleb base their calculations on?

_____

_____

Check out Jeremiah 17:7-8 to see what the rich reward is for those who trust God.

b. Due to unbelief, Israel wandered 40 years in the wilderness. But what happened to the 10 men who turned the people against Moses? (See Numbers 14:36-38.)

_____

_____

_____

c. Have you been living more in faith and humility, or in unbelief and pride? What fruit from your life proves that?

_____

_____

_____

_____

_____

Voice of the Ages

"*Pride* renders faith *impossible*. ...Is it any wonder that our faith is so feeble when pride still reigns so much, and we have scarce learned even to long or pray for humility as the most needful and blessed part of salvation? ...It is the *humility* that brings a soul to be nothing before God that also removes every hindrance to faith..."
—Andrew Murray[1]

UNBELIEF

In Scripture, when the word *unbelief* is used, it almost always means "disobedient." Both words, *unbelief* and *disobedient*, are taken from the Greek word *apeitheia*. This word communicates "the condition of being unpersuadable"; it also means "obstinacy and obstinate rejection of the will of God, hence *disobedience*."[2]

3. The Israelites who left Egypt believed in God, but they *lacked faith* in Him to fulfill His promise to bring them into the Promised Land. As a result, they died in their unbelief—they fell far short of the destiny God had planned for them.

   a. When we choose *not* to believe God's Word, what are we actually communicating to God in our hearts? What does the example of Israel's unbelief and God's response speak to you?

   _____

   _____

   _____

4. The longer you look at something, the bigger it becomes. So instead of focusing on your problems and magnifying them, God wants us to focus on and magnify *Him*. This means exalting and praising Him for His awesomeness and celebrating the wonderful things He's already done.

   a. How big is God in your eyes? Read these passages and describe any new insights the Holy Spirit reveals to you about the immensity of our Maker.

   Nehemiah 9:6-7 • Psalm 95:3-6; 104 • Hebrews 1:3; 11:3

   _____

   _____

   _____

   _____

   b. Take a moment and write a paragraph of personal praise to the Lord who loves you.

   _____

   _____

   _____

   Check out Psalm 29:2; 57:5; 145.

> If we *believe* we are no different than those who haven't been liberated by the grace of God, we'll live as they do—in the ordinary. We'll live the way we were trained, captives of this world's system. However, if we allow the **Word of God** to change how we see ourselves, and we *truly believe it in our hearts*, then we'll begin to live like heaven's royalty—the realm of the extraordinary!

JOHN BEVERE
adapted from chapter 13

Heaven's
APPEAL

> The law of the Lord is perfect, reviving the soul. The statutes of the Lord are trustworthy, *making wise* the simple. The precepts of the Lord are right, *giving joy* to the heart. The commands of the Lord are radiant, *giving light* to the eyes.
> —Psalm 19:7-8 NIV

5. As we learned previously, *faith has a language*: It is bold, confident and absent of doubt, indecisiveness, and uncertainty. Words of faith are not based on head knowledge, but on *heart* revelation of God's Word and the truth of who you are in Him.

a. *Get quiet before the Lord* and take a few moments to examine your thought life and the words you speak about yourself and your circumstances. Are you thinking and speaking the language of faith or fear?

_____

_____

_____

b. **Check out** these passages and describe what they say about your true identity:

1 Peter 2:9 • Romans 8:16-17 • Galatians 4:4-7

_____

_____

_____

c. **Ponder these promises** and explain why you need to live your life looking through *the lens of God's Word* instead of focusing on circumstances.

Psalm 119:89,152 • Matthew 5:18; 24:35

_____

_____

_____

FASCINATING FACT: THE ULTIMATE RULER

The Bible, meaning "The Book," contains two portions: the Old Testament, which the early Christians claimed—along with the Jews—and the New Testament, which the early Christians produced in spite of the Jews. The Old Testament *promised*; the New Testament *fulfilled*.

The word for the special place these books occupy is *canon*. This term from the Greek language originally meant "a measuring rod" or "ruler." It was a standard for judging something straight. So this idea transferred to a list of books that constituted the standard or "rule," for believers.[3] It was agreed that these books were "God-breathed" and contain the authority of God. Each have a self-evidencing quality—they have always exercised, and continue to exercise, an unparalleled power to change the lives of men.[4] For Christians, they have become the **ruler** by which a believer determines how his life measures up to the Master, Jesus Christ.

According to noted historian Josephus, the compilation of Old Testament books is believed to have been done by Ezra around 450 B.C.[5] The books that make up the New Testament today were chosen for the fundamental reason that they were written by an apostle, or at least by a man who had direct contact with the circle of the apostles. It was both the councils in North Africa at Hippo (393 A.D.) and at Carthage (397 A.D.) that formally ratified and published the list of the 27 books of the New Testament as we know them today.[6]

6. Next to the *Word of God* is the unsurpassed supremacy of the **name of Jesus**. Indeed, there is inherent, empowering grace *through faith* in His name! Read John 14:13-14; 15:7-8 and Philippians 2:9-10 and write what these scriptures speak to your heart.

_____

_____

_____

_____

_____

_____

_____

Voice of the Ages

"The possibilities involved in [Jesus'] name are beyond our understanding. When Jesus says, **whatever you ask the Father in my name**, He is giving us a signed check on the resources of heaven, and asking us to fill it in. What a privilege.

If you are in need of healing, begin a study of the resources of Jesus, in order to obtain a measure of the wealth which that name holds for you today. It is yours to use today. Jesus said so. Only believe and begin to use His name in prayer today."

—**T.L. Osborn**[7]

[word in brackets added for clarity]

POWER

The noun form of the word "power" in Greek is *dunamis*. Its universal meaning is "**inherent** *power*, *strength* and *ability* **residing in a thing** by virtue of its nature, or which a person or thing exerts and puts forth."[8]

7. According to Ephesians 1:19, there is *unlimited,* immeasurable *power* in us who *believe,* or have *faith,* in the completed work of Christ. *Meditate on the message* of these eye-opening truths. Let them really sink into your soul and spirit.

> For out of His **fullness** (abundance) *we have all received* [all had a share and we were all supplied with] one grace after another and spiritual blessing upon spiritual blessing and even favor upon favor and gift [heaped] upon gift.
>
> **—John 1:16 AMP**
>
> And God has put all things under the authority of Christ, and he gave him this authority for the benefit of the church. And the church is his body; it is **filled** *by Christ,* who fills everything everywhere with his presence.
>
> **—Ephesians 1:22-23 NLT**
>
> For in Him the whole fullness of Deity (the Godhead) continues to dwell in bodily form [giving complete expression of the divine nature]. And you are in Him, made full and having come to **fullness** of life [*in Christ you too are filled with the Godhead*—Father, Son and Holy Spirit—and reach full spiritual stature]...
>
> **—Colossians 2:9-10 AMP**

a. What is the Holy Spirit revealing to you about the *fullness* of Christ in you?

_____

_____

b. Why do you think the enemy is afraid of you finding this out?

_____

_____

c. Read Romans 8:11 and write what it speaks to your heart:

_____

_____

"We should be the people the world is seeking to learn from. We should be the ones *influencing* the world because the One who created the gorgeous Rocky Mountains, paints the beautiful sunsets, and created the wonderful sea creatures *lives on the inside of us!*"

JOHN BEVERE
adapted from session 8

8. As a son or daughter of the Great Creator, God has positioned you to *rule in life* and be an *influencer of righteousness*—He has empowered you with His grace and given you gifts to make an eternal difference in the lives of others.

...All who receive God's abundant grace and are freely put right with him will *rule in life* through Christ.
—Romans 5:17 TEV

a. What is your God-defined *sphere of influence* that He has given you? How are you using your influence to bring the reality of His kingdom to others?

_____

_____

_____

b. Name one obvious way you can know for certain that you're influencing people in an extraordinary way. (See page 143 in the book.) In light of this, who do you know you are influencing?

_____

_____

c. *Get quiet before the Lord*. Ask Him to show you some new, creative ways to indelibly impact others for Him using your gifts. Write what He reveals.

_____

_____

9. If the *fullness* of God has been given to us in the form of grace, why are so many Christians *not* enjoying an overcoming, godly life? Why are we not the wisest and most creative people on earth, healing the sick, and freeing the captives? Because we need a deeper revelation of God's amazing power available to us through faith.

Meditate on the message of Ephesians 3:20, asking the Holy Spirit to deposit the power and reality of it in your heart:

Now to Him Who, by (in consequence of) the [action of His] power that is at work *within us*, is *able* to [carry out His purpose and] do *superabundantly*, far over and above all that we [dare] ask or think [**infinitely beyond** our highest prayers, desires, thoughts, hopes, or dreams]—to Him be glory...
—**Amplified**
[includes part of Ephesians 3:21]

God can do anything, you know—**far more** than you could ever imagine or guess or request in your wildest dreams! He does it *not* by pushing us around but by working *within us*, his Spirit deeply and gently within us.

—**The Message**

Now glory be to God, who by his mighty power at work *within us* is *able* to do far more than we would ever dare to ask or even dream of—**infinitely beyond** our highest prayers, desires, thoughts, or hopes.

—**The Living Bible**

a. What new understanding is the Holy Spirit showing you about His power?

_____

_____

b. Describe one of your "highest" desires, hopes, or dreams. Have you ever *dared* to ask God for it? If not, why? How does your new insight of this verse change things?

_____

_____

"You are an heir of the King of the universe! You are one of a royal company of people. You are set apart as God's ruling class of sons and daughters. We must know this and believe it in our hearts, for it's only then that we access the power of the divine nature and bring glory to our Father in heaven. **It's all about believing the truth** about ourselves; for if we do not believe, we do not have access to the amazing provision of the grace of God."

JOHN BEVERE
adapted from chapter 13

10. God says that He's ABLE to do *superabundantly, infinitely beyond* all that you could dare ask or think, but if we don't see evidence of this type of power operating in our lives, there is a good chance that we are *limiting* God in some way. (See pages 146 in the book.)

a. What limits the power of God working in and through you—what determines the size of your "container" or capacity to house God's power?

_____

b. What has kept you from praying, imagining and believing God for more?

_____

_____

c. To a great degree, what have you potentially been more influenced and motivated by?

_____

_____

_____

11. People in the early church didn't struggle to believe they had God's power working in and through them because Jesus had been their role model. They had seen firsthand what He could do and didn't have the *experiences* of others to discourage their faith.

Heaven's APPEAL

Last of all I want to remind you that your strength must come from the Lord's mighty power *within you*.

—Ephesians 6:10 TLB

a. How has the enemy fought tirelessly to hold back the truth of God's grace from being taught in the church today? (See page 146 in the book.)

_____

_____

_____

b. What *excuses* for the power of God not manifesting today have you believed? Are they scriptural?

_____

_____

c. *Get quiet before the Lord.* Ask Him, "Lord, have I bought into any unscriptural teachings or theories that are robbing me of faith? If so, what are they?" Write what He reveals.

_____

_____

Heaven's APPEAL

Don't let others *spoil your faith* and *joy* with their *philosophies*, their wrong and shallow answers built on men's thoughts and ideas, instead of on what Christ has said.

—Colossians 2:8 TLB

12. If the enemy can keep you bound to the memories and feelings of a *former experience* instead of focusing on the truth of God's Word, he can effectively stop you from growing into a powerful and productive believer.

a. What former experience(s) comes to mind that is hindering you from truly believing God's Word, and consequently, keeping your faith from growing?

_____

_____

_____

_____

_____

b. Is there a disappointing experience of a *family member* or *close friend* that you have allowed to supersede the truth and stifle the growth of your faith? If so, what is it?

_____

_____

Surrender these situations to God in prayer. Pour your heart out to Him—ask Him to heal the hurts and disappointments and remove the fears you are dealing with. If you have been struggling to understand why something happened, ask Him for grace to enable your mind to rest and trust Him.

Voice of the Ages

"If I construct my faith on my *experience*, I produce that most unscriptural type, an isolated life, my eyes fixed on my own whiteness. ...Measure every type of experience by our Lord Himself. We cannot do anything pleasing to God unless we deliberately build on the presupposition [faith] of the Atonement.[9]

If your faith is in *experiences*, anything that happens is likely to upset that faith; but nothing can ever upset God or the almighty Reality of Redemption; base your faith on that, and you are as eternally secure as God. When once you get into personal contact with Jesus Christ, you will never be moved again."[10]

—Oswald Chambers
[word in brackets added for clarity]

UNVEIL YOUR HERO

A professional surfer turns his travel opportunities into mission trips as he reaches out to the poor and downtrodden and visits the sick.

Light is being spread in our world by **Toby**...

the bottom line

God's grace is His power. It is accessed through the "pipeline" of our faith and works within us to do exceedingly above and beyond all that we could dare to ask or think. Through faith, we not only access the grace to be saved, but also to walk in holiness, manifest His kingdom, and secure every promise that is ours through Christ.

REPROGRAM Your Hard Drive

...If you *abide* in **My word** [hold fast to My teachings and live in accordance with them], you are truly My disciples. And you will know the Truth, and *the Truth will set you free.*
—John 8:31-32 AMP

Is your life *busy*? Most of us are being pulled in more directions than we would like, trying to juggle work, relationships, bill paying, housekeeping, grocery shopping, car repairs, and everything else under the sun. Finding time to feed our spirits the nourishment of Scripture is definitely a challenge, but it's a challenge we can and *must* overcome by the grace of God.

The moment you repent of your sin and invite Christ into your life, you are saved and rescued from the devil's dominion. But while your spirit is immediately made alive and new, your thinking still needs work—in some cases, *a lot of work*.

Think about it. Your mind is the birth place of every action you make. Proverbs 23:7 says, "For as [a man] thinks in his heart, so is he..." (AMP, words in brackets added for clarity). If your *actions* are not in line with God's Word, it is because your *thinking* is not in line with God's Word. This is why reprogramming is critical.

John G. Lake, renowned minister of healing to Africa and abroad during the early 1900s, said...

> "If there is any particular area where as a rule Christians are weak, it is in the *consecration of their minds*. Christians seem to feel as if they are not to exercise any control over the mind, so it seems to run at random, just like the mind of the world.
>
> Real Christianity is marked by the pureness, the holiness of the thoughts of man; and if the kind of Christianity you have does not produce in your mind real holiness, real purity, real sweetness, real truth, then it is a poor brand. **Change it** right away.
>
> There is relief for the unsanctified mind. Submit your mind to the Lord Jesus Christ to be remolded by the Holy Spirit, so that it becomes the *pure channel* of a holy nature."[11]

Realize that reprogramming the hard drive of your mind with the truth of God's Word is *not* optional—it's *mandatory*. Only God's Word in the hands of the Holy Spirit, who lives in you, has the inherent power to change your life—nothing else.

"God's Word is not merely letters on paper...it's alive. Believe and draw near, for it longs to dance in your heart and whisper to you in the night."

LISA BEVERE[12]

Read the following passages and write how you are stirred by them:

Psalm 119:11 • 2 Timothy 3:16 • Romans 12:2 • Ephesians 4:23-24 • Joshua 1:8 • Colossians 3:16

_____

_____

_____

_____

Reading the Word is wonderful. But to really build your faith and begin thinking like Jesus thinks, *meditation* is the key. Ask the Holy Spirit to give you revelation knowledge, and think about and allow God's *principles* and *promises* to be the new lens in which you operate from.

Remember, *grace* is God's power to live like Jesus and be fruitful. The only way to access grace is through the *pipeline of faith*, and building the pipeline of "...faith comes from listening to the Good News—the Good News about Christ" (Romans 10:17 TLB).

It's time to examine your fields! (Refer to the graph on page 153 of the book.) What aspects of your life are not connected to the "water" of God's grace? In other words, what areas of the Word do you have a hard time believing? Is it healing? Walking in holiness? Tithing and giving offerings? Overcoming fear? Receiving the baptism of the Holy Spirit? Trusting God for protection and provision? Whatever you struggle to believe is the area where your pipeline of faith needs to be built!

THE LORD IS SHOWING ME I NEED TO BUILD A "PIPELINE" OF FAITH IN THESE AREAS:

_____

_____

_____

_____

_____

_____

Voice of the Ages

"We must realize the value of **God's Word** and the value of quiet meditation in the Word. The most deeply spiritual men and women I know give time to meditation in the Word of God. You cannot develop spiritual wisdom without meditation. ...Take time to meditate in God's Word. Shut yourself in alone with your own spirit, with the world shut out. Begin by taking 10 or 15 minutes daily for meditation; that isn't much. Begin the development of your own spirit. Begin—and then it will grow. Begin _taking time_."

—Kenneth Hagin[13]

One by one, begin a systematic study of these topics. All you need is a good Bible concordance, like _Strong's Exhaustive Concordance of the Bible_, one or more understandable version of the Bible, a notebook and a pen. The Holy Spirit is your Teacher who permanently abides within you. Invite Him in at the onset of every study and watch how His Word comes alive like never before!

FOR FURTHER STUDY

BEWARE OF PRIDE
Psalm 10:2; 119:21
Proverbs 11:2; 16:18; 21:4
Proverbs 3:7; 26:12
Isaiah 5:21; Romans 12:16

POWER IN JESUS' NAME
Mark 16:17; Luke 24:47
John 15:16; 20:31

BE A GODLY INFLUENCE
Matthew 5:13-16
1 Timothy 4:12
Titus 2:7

Acts 3:16; 4:12; 16:18
James 5:14; 1 John 5:14-15

Journal
Your Journey

Night and day we pray most earnestly that we may see
you again and *supply what is lacking in your faith.*
—1 Thessalonians 3:10 NIV

EYE-OPENERS
Are you becoming more firmly established in the faith? Pause for a moment
and revisit some of the eye-opening truths the Holy Spirit has made real to
you; write what He brings to mind.

_____

_____

_____

_____

_____

_____

REVOLUTIONARY YOU
How is the Lord stirring you to search and study His Word more? Is He
prompting you to build new *pipelines* of faith to access His grace? Ask Him
to show you a plan of how to fulfill this.

_____

_____

_____

_____

_____

_____

PRAYER FOR REVELATION
*Lord, may the eyes of my heart be flooded with light, so that I can know
and understand the hope to which You have called me and how rich is Your
glorious inheritance in the saints, Your set-apart ones. Help me to know and
understand in my heart and by personal experience the immeasurable, unlimited and surpassing greatness of Your power in and for me, as demonstrated
in the working of Your mighty strength, which You exerted in Christ when You
raised Him from the dead. Thank You, Lord...in Jesus' name, Amen.*

[based on Ephesians 1:18-20 AMP]

NOTES

1. Andrew Murray, *Humility* (Fort Washington, PA: CLC Publications, 1997) pp. 73-74. 2. Adapted from *Vine's Complete Expository Dictionary — New Testament Words*, W. E. Vine (Nashville, TN: Thomas Nelson, Inc. 1996) pp. 61, 173, 649. 3. Adapted from Bruce L. Shelly, *Church History in Plain Language* (Dallas, TX: Word Publishing, Inc.) pp. 73-74. 4. Ibid., p. 76. 5. Adapted from *Halley's Bible Handbook* (Grand Rapids, MI: Zondervan Publishing House, 1965) p. 405. 6. See note 3, pp. 77, 83. 7. T.L. Osborn, *Healing the Sick* (Tulsa OK: Harrison House, 1992) p. 30. 8. *Thayer's Greek-English Lexicon of the New Testament*, Joseph H. Thayer (Grand Rapids, MI: Baker Book House Company, 1977) p. 159. 9. Oswald Chambers, *My Utmost for His Highest* (Uhrichsville, OH: Barbour Publishing, Inc., MCMXCVII) p. 283. 10. Ibid., p. 338. 11. Dr. John G. Lake, *Spiritual Hunger, The God-Men and Other Sermons* (Dallas, TX: Christ for the Nations, Inc. 1979) pp. 45-46. 12. Lisa Bevere, *Kissed the Girls and Made Them Cry* (Nashville, TN: Thomas Nelson, Inc., 2002) p. 139. 13. Kenneth E. Hagin, *Exceedingly Growing Faith* (Tulsa, OK: Rhema Bible Church, 2006) pp. 59, 61.

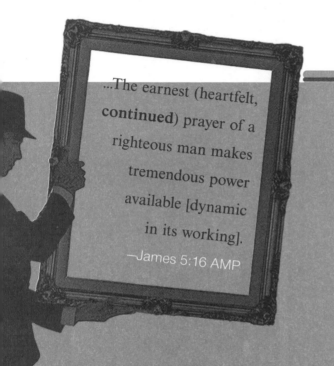

...The earnest (heartfelt, **continued**) prayer of a righteous man makes tremendous power available [dynamic in its working].

—James 5:16 AMP

xtraordin

True Faith Is Relentless

Please refer to chapter 14 in the *Extraordinary* book, along with session 9 of the teaching series.

> "Everything we receive from the Lord is through **faith**. God does not respond to our need; He responds to our faith. This principle applies to all areas of life, including our ability to walk in holiness, live creatively, apprehend wisdom or inspired ideas, receive healing or deliverance from habitual behavior, etc. In short, faith is needed to receive *anything* heaven has provided for our lives, or, more importantly, for reaching our world with the Gospel. We cannot minister effectively unless it is done in faith."

JOHN BEVERE
adapted from chapter 14

Heaven's APPEAL

1. When Jesus lived on earth, He encountered people from all walks of life. Many of them physically touched Him, but not everyone who touched Him received from Him.

   a. Explain what consistently *grieved* Jesus and what consistently pleased Him.

> But without faith it is impossible to please Him, for he who comes to God must believe that He is, and that He is a rewarder of those who diligently seek Him.
> —Hebrews 11:6 NKJV

_____

_____

_____

_____

_____

_____

_____

b. James 1:6-8 alerts us of the main obstacle to receiving from God and the consequences that result. What is that obstacle and what does this scripture mean, in your own words?

_____

_____

_____

2. In each miraculous example presented in this session, there's a common theme that must not be overlooked. Read Matthew 15:28, Mark 5:34 and 10:52 and identify Jesus' recurring words, declaring the reason each person received their healing. What does this speak to you?

_____

_____

_____

Heaven's APPEAL

Fight the good fight of the faith. **Take hold** of the eternal life to which you were called when you made your good confession in the presence of many witnesses.
—1 Timothy 6:12 NIV

3. Read the story of the Canaanite (Greek) woman who sought after Jesus to heal her demon-possessed daughter in Matthew 15:21-28 and Mark 7:24-30.

a. Based on her request, how would you describe her character?

_____

_____

_____

_____

Voice of the Ages

"The *strength of faith* is not out there when you are winning the battle. The strength of faith is in the matter of *decisions*. Gideon's faith showed when he said, 'I won't quit. Even though I had 32,000 reduced to 10,000, I won't quit.' When that was reduced to 300, he said, 'I still won't quit.' ... Faith is courage. When you are reduced, you don't quit. Then when you are reduced again, you don't quit. When God says, 'Go against a major enemy,' you go. And you win. The victory is the fruit of faith."
—**Dr. Lester Sumrall**[1]

b. In what ways can you personally identify with her situation, and what can you learn from her example and apply in your life?

_____

_____

_____

_____

_____

_____

_____

_____

_____

_____

PERSISTENT DETERMINED RELENTLESS

To *persist* literally means "to stand or be fixed." It signifies "continuing steadily and firmly in the pursuit of any business or course commenced; to persevere." Similarly, *determination* is "the act of deciding a question in the mind; having a firm resolution, settled purpose and absolute direction to a certain end."[2] Another word for persistent and determined is *relentless*.

4. When Jesus traveled and ministered, large crowds gathered and followed Him everywhere He went. This was also true of His journey from Jericho to Jerusalem—the day He met the blind man named Bartimaeus.

Check out the story of Bartimaeus in Mark 10:46-52.

a. Why do you think Jesus asked Bartimaeus, "What do you want Me to do for you?"

_____

_____

_____

_____

_____

b. There were probably others in the crowd who had needs, yet only Bartimaeus' need was met. Why? What did he do to get his need met, and what can you learn from him?

_____

_____

_____

_____

_____

"So Jesus said, 'Have faith in God' (Mark 11:22). ...Here is the sentence in the Greek: 'And answering, the Jesus says to them: 'Have you *faith of God?*' That is the actual, word-for-word translation from the original.

Then the Master went on to tell them that *if they had such a faith*, not only would a little fig tree dry up at the exercise of such faith, but that mountains could be removed and cast into the sea. The lesson was that of the irresistible power of the faith that was the faith *of God*. It was indeed mountain-moving faith.

...Generally we interpret that scripture, 'Have faith in God,' to mean that we have confidence in God's power to move a mountain. We say in our hearts, 'If only I have faith enough *in* God; if only I can believe hard enough; and if only I can get doubt out of my heart, then God will move that mountain.'

You are trying to do the impossible. Your faith would never be strong enough or pure enough for that, though you were to struggle for a million years. ...There is a great deal of difference between what we call *the faith of man in God*, and the *faith of God* that is imparted to man. Such faith is not the child of effort, neither is it born of struggle. If it is the faith *of* God, then we get it *from* Him, and not from our mental attitudes or affirmations.

...God deals to *every* man his measure of faith (see Romans 12:3). ...God *gives the faith*. He measures it out! ...Faith *chases death away* from its vigil over bodies, *and* it *brings back the life* that had fled. Faith! *God's Faith!*"

—**Dr. Charles S. Price**[3]

5. Probably one of the most powerful passages connecting faith and the demonstration of God's kingdom power on earth is Mark 11:22-24. Look up these verses in a few versions of the Bible and write out the one that ignites the greatest fire of faith in your heart.

a. MARK 11:22-24

_____

_____

_____

_____

_____

_____

b. List the step-by-step instruction Jesus gives for dealing with a mountain of adversity.

_____

_____

_____

c. What else is the Holy Spirit revealing to you about this passage?

_____

_____

_____

> " Jesus makes it clear that **when we pray** and command something to be done, that's when we believe and *receive* what we've asked for. As far as we are concerned, *it will be done the moment we speak* forth our command.
> It doesn't matter what our eyes see or our senses tell us; we have a more sure report to believe—the Word of our God. "
>
> **JOHN BEVERE**
> adapted from chapter 14

6. How long has it been since you *knew that you knew* God heard and answered your prayer?

a. *Meditate on the message* of these powerful promises regarding God's faithfulness:

> If you belong to the Lord, reverence him; for everyone who does this has everything he needs. Even strong young lions sometimes go hungry, but those of us who reverence the Lord will *never lack any good thing*.
>
> **—Psalm 34:9-10 TLB**

> And God is able to make all grace (every favor and earthly blessing) come to you *in abundance*, so that you may always and under all circumstances and whatever the need be self-sufficient [possessing enough to require no aid or support and furnished *in abundance* for every good work and charitable donation].
>
> **—2 Corinthians 9:8 AMP**

> And my God will liberally supply (fill to the full) your every need according to His riches in glory in Christ Jesus.
>
> **—Philippians 4:19 AMP**

What is the Lord speaking to you through these passages?

_____

_____

_____

Check out more promises on God's provision at the end of this session.

b. Take a few moments to jot down some **specific needs** you have. Then go to God in prayer. Thank Him for the awesome things He's *already done*, share the specific needs you *presently* have, and thank Him now for faithfully answering them.

LORD, HERE ARE SOME OF MY SPECIFIC NEEDS...

_____

_____

_____

_____

Thank You, Father, for faithfully supplying all my needs!

Voice of the Ages

"Take courage! God often allows us to go through difficulties to purify our souls and to teach us to rely on Him more (1 Peter 1:6-7). So offer Him your problems unceasingly, and ask Him for the strength to overcome them.

Talk to Him often. Forget Him as seldom as possible. Praise Him. When the difficulties are at their worst, go to Him humbly and lovingly—as a child goes to a loving father— and ask for the help you need from His *grace*."

—Brother Lawrence[4]

7. After reading the detailed account of the "Colorado Hayman Fire" and how John and his staff handled the situation, how has your faith been stirred? How can you apply this example to a situation you are currently facing?

_____

_____

_____

_____

_____

Heaven's APPEAL

Be assured and understand that the trial and proving of your faith bring out endurance and steadfastness and patience.

—James 1:3 AMP

8. One of the blessings of developing *relentless faith* is the development of *perseverance* and *endurance*—key qualities we need in order to inherit the promises of God. (See Hebrews 10:35-36, James 1:4 and Galatians 6:9.)

a. What are you to do when the enemy's after you? First Peter 5:8-9 reveals the answer; what is it, and how does this scripture call you to action?

_____

_____

_____

_____

FASCINATING FACT: PERSISTENCE PAYS OFF
FROM THE DIARY OF JOHN WESLEY . . . [5]

Sunday, A.M., May 5	Preached in St. Anne's. Was asked not to come back anymore.
Sunday, P.M., May 5	Preached in St. John's. Deacons said, "Get out and stay out."
Sunday, A.M., May 12	Preached in St. Jude's. Can't go back there either.
Sunday, A.M., May 19	Preached in St. Somebody Else's. Deacons called special meeting and said I couldn't return.
Sunday, P.M., May 19	Preached on street. Kicked off street.
Sunday, A.M., May 26	Preached in meadow. Chased out of meadow as bull was turned loose during service.
Sunday, A.M., June 2	Preached out at the edge of town. Kicked off the highway.
Sunday, P.M., June 2	Afternoon, preached in a pasture. *Ten thousand people came out to hear me.*

9. Jesus reveals in John 10:10 that the enemy's aim is to *steal, kill* and *destroy* anything he can. But He came that we "...may have and enjoy life, and have it in *abundance* (to the full, till it overflows)" (AMP).

a. What has Satan been trying to steal, kill and destroy in your life? How are you standing against him?

_____

_____

_____

_____

If you don't have a plan, ask the Lord to give you one and write what He shares.

b. Is there a situation in your church, job or community in which the enemy is trying to bring death and destruction? If so, explain what it is and ask the Lord for a specific plan of action to *stand in faith* against him.

_____

_____

_____

Heaven's
APPEAL

Yet we have the same **spirit of faith** as he had who wrote, I have believed, and therefore have I spoken. We too believe, and therefore *we speak*.
—2 Corinthians 4:13 AMP

10. In the story of the woman who had an issue of blood for 12 years, the Bible states that she was "...saying to herself, 'If I just touch his clothes, I will get well'" (Mark 5:27-28 TEV).

a. What kind of things are you *saying to yourself* about the problem you're facing? How do you need to change your words to reflect a spirit of *faith*?

_____

_____

_____

Voice
of the Ages

"The key to overcoming sickness and problems is the **God-kind of faith**—believing with the heart and confessing with the mouth. Our lips can make us victors or keep us captives. We can fill our words with faith or we can fill our words with doubt. ...Our faith will never rise above the words of our lips. ... Thoughts may come and may persist in staying. But if we refuse to put those thoughts into words, they die unborn. Cultivate the habit of thinking big things. Learn to use words that will react upon your own spirit. *Faith's confessions create realities.*"
—**Kenneth E. Hagin**[6]

_____

_____

_____

_____

_____

b. Your words are extremely important. Read the following scriptures and write what they mean to you:

Proverbs 18:20-21 • Psalm 19:14 • James 3:1-12

_____

_____

_____

11. In Isaiah 60:1-5, we get a glimpse of the *extraordinary* life God has called us to live, especially in these last days. Read this passage and answer the questions below.

a. How will God's glory manifest upon you and others—where will it come from?

_____

_____

_____

_____

Heaven's
APPEAL

So what makes you think God won't step in and work justice for his chosen people, who *continue* to cry out for help? Won't he stick up for them? I assure you, he will. He will not drag his feet. But how much of that kind of **persistent faith** will the Son of Man find on the earth when he returns?
—Luke 18:7-8 The Message

b. What will be the tangible results of His glorious power and presence in your life?

_____

_____

c. What do you think is holding back this radiant manifestation?

_____

_____

"Are you seeing how important faith is and why the Bible tells us it is 'impossible to please God' without it? We're called to the extraordinary, but we can't attain it without faith! Let's shake off our grave clothes. We are not people of this world. We have God's *divine nature* and are sons and daughters of light with exceeding great power within us. The devil is no match for the glorious church Isaiah prophesied. *Now* is the time for the church to arise and go forward relentlessly in faith and bring heaven to earth, in our lives and in the world of our influence!"

JOHN BEVERE
adapted from chapter 14

UNVEIL YOUR HERO

...did not make the cut for his high school basketball team

Michael Jordan–6 World Championships

the bottom line

God responds to our faith, not our need. Relentless, persistent faith is a determination to lay hold of God's promises through believing and speaking the Word and through Spirit-led actions. We must use our authority to bring heaven to earth.

Journal Your Journey

> Don't tolerate what Jesus paid such a high price to free you from. Don't tolerate death, don't tolerate destruction, and don't tolerate theft. *Speak directly to the opposition* and *command it to move into the sea!* Speak from your authority of being one with Him, joint heirs with Him, ruling in this life through the abundance of grace.

JOHN BEVERE
adapted from chapter 14 and session 9

EYE-OPENERS

Undoubtedly, your extraordinary journey continues to yield new discoveries. What revelations about *relentless faith* and perseverance is the Holy Spirit showing you?

_____

_____

_____

_____

_____

_____

REVOLUTIONARY YOU

In light of all the truths you've pondered, what new goals are you challenged to establish to help develop a deeper determination in your faith?

_____

_____

_____

_____

_____

PRAYER FOR PERSISTENCE

Lord, forgive me for my lack of faith and for praying passively as a result. Help me to become grounded in Your Word and begin to consistently and passionately pray Your promises instead of just talking to You about my problems. Give me Your grace to ask, and keep on asking; to seek and keep on seeking; to knock and keep on knocking on Your heart's door until I see it opened and the manifestation of Your promise come to pass. I love You, Lord, and I thank You for developing in me a true, relentless faith...in Jesus' name, Amen.

[based on Matthew 7:7-8]

All of Heaven
IS BACKING YOU!

Behold! I have given you *authority* and *power* to trample
upon serpents and scorpions, and [physical and mental strength
and ability] over all the power that the enemy [possesses];
and nothing shall in any way harm you.
—Luke 10:19 AMP

Imagine a six-foot-four, 250-pound state highway patrol officer. In his muscular physical stature and rugged personality he has power, but his power is *limited*. His greatest power is invisible and comes from his position of authority—the authority of the state he represents.

Let's say this officer identifies the driver of an 18-wheeler exceeding the speed limit by 20 mph in a school zone. As a servant of the state, he must **enforce** the law to protect the people. When he turns his siren on to pull the driver over, it is the power of his authority that makes the driver stop, not his physical strength.

Similarly, God has given you power as a believer. However, not only has He given you power, but He has also given you authority. In fact, you could say that all of heaven is backing you. And as a servant of the Kingdom of God, it is your duty to enforce the law, which is His will defined in His Word, in order to protect and rescue the lives of people.

T.L. Osborn personally witnessed the miraculous healings of multitudes as he and his wife, Daisy, traveled in more than 70 nations of the world. Examine this excerpt concerning our position of power and authority in his classic book *Healing the Sick*:

> "You and I must look about us and see our position today. The believer today has the *same* power and authority that the believers had then, if we will use it.
>
> ...We are ordained to represent Christ in this life (John 15:16). We are to work the works of Jesus. We are to manifest His faith and His love. We are to speak the words of the Father which Christ gave us to speak (John 17:7,14).
>
> ...Let us take our place as authorized ambassadors for Christ, acting in Christ's stead (2 Corinthians 5:20). ...Ambassadors never doubt that the country which they represent will *back up* their word. They know it will. The very title of their office implies that.
>
> ...We should assume our place as a child of God, as an heir of God; and with this equal power with Christ, according to John 14:12, take our place, acting representatively in Jesus' stead, bringing to the world the blessings promised by our heavenly Father.
>
> ...God wants us to face our world and to meet her need today as Peter did in his day. This is *our* day of ministry. Roll up your sleeves and go set the captives free. Open the blind eyes, unstop the deaf ears, and break the bands of Satan and his sicknesses. The world is depending on you. You have this power in you. It is given to you by God. **Act on it** today. Begin today, acting in Jesus' name—in His stead."[7]

Write down any "explosions" of truth the Holy Spirit is revealing in your spirit through T.L. Osborn's excerpt.

_____

_____

_____

_____

_____

_____

MEDITATE on the MESSAGE...

What is man that You are mindful of him, and the son of man that You visit him? For You have made him a little lower than the angels, and You have crowned him with glory and honor (NKJV). You have put him in charge of everything you made; *everything is put under his authority* (TLB).

—Psalm 8:4-6

The heaven of heavens is for God, but he put us in charge of the earth.

—Psalm 115:16 The Message

Read Genesis 1:26-28 and chapter 3—the account of man first receiving his authority and dominion and how he lost it. What new insights is the Holy Spirit revealing to you?

_____

_____

_____

_____

_____

Jesus, the Son of Man and Last Adam, regained man's authority and dominion through His death, burial and resurrection. In Matthew 28:18-19, He said, "...**All authority** has been given to Me in heaven and on earth. Go therefore and make disciples of all the nations...." What is the significant connection between these two statements, and what does it mean to you as a believer?

_____

_____

_____

_____

_____

_____

Read Ephesians 1:15 through 2:7 to get a good snapshot of your position in Christ.

According to Ephesians 1:20, where is Jesus right now?

_____

As a member of the body of Christ, where are you?

And where is Satan and his demonic horde in relation to Jesus? How about in relation to *you*?

What new perspective does this give you as a believer?

> 66 This is what it takes to live extraordinarily—this is what God has called us to do. We need to be people who know that heaven backs us. When you have the heart and mind of God in a situation and you're doing His will, nothing can stand in your way! 99
>
> **JOHN BEVERE**
> adapted from session 9

FOR FURTHER STUDY

GOD WILL PROVIDE
Exodus 23:25
Psalm 31:19; 33:18-19; 84:11
Malachi 3:10-12
Luke 6:38
2 Corinthians 9:8-11

PERSEVERANCE/ENDURANCE
1 Corinthians 15:58
Galatians 5:1
Philippians 1:27
Colossians 1:9-12
James 5:11,17-18

AUTHORITY
Matthew 16:19; 18:18-20
Romans 13:1-3
Hebrews 13:17

1. Dr. Lester Sumrall, *Faith Can Change Your World* (South Bend, IN: Sumrall Publishing, 1999) pp. 157-158. 2. Adapted from *Noah Webster's First Edition of an American Dictionary of the English Language* (1828), Republished in facsimile edition by Foundation for American Christian Education (San Francisco, CA 1995). 3. Charles S. Price, *The Real Faith: Original Pentecostal Classics Edition* (Wichita, KS: EM Publications, 2008) pp. 71-77. 4. Brother Lawrence, *The Practice of the Presence of God* (New Kensington, PA: Whitaker House, 1982) p. 54. 5. Illustrations on *Perseverance* (www. sermonillustrations.com, retrieved 6/2/09). 6. Kenneth E. Hagin, *Exceedingly Growing Faith* (Tulsa, OK: Rhema Bible Church, 2006) pp. 101-102. 7. T.L. Osborn, *Healing the Sick* (Tulsa, OK: Harrison House, 1992) pp. 168, 170-172, 174.

NOTES

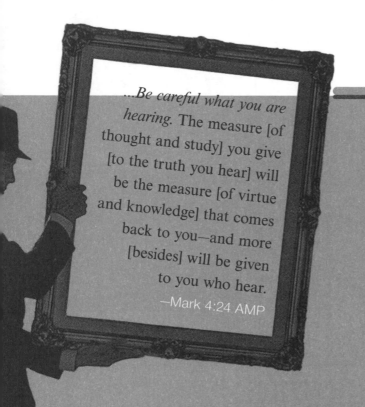

...Be careful what you are hearing. The measure [of thought and study] you give [to the truth you hear] will be the measure [of virtue and knowledge] that comes back to you—and more [besides] will be given to you who hear.

—Mark 4:24 AMP

xtraordin

What Are You Listening To? 10

Please refer to chapter 15 in the *Extraordinary* book, along with session 10 of the teaching series.

> "The divine nature has been imparted to us! We have extraordinary potential! But we have to *feed correct knowledge into our minds*, which will eventually be deposited in our hearts and deeply believed. Then we will say to any adversity, 'Be pulled up by the roots,' and it will obey us. Even though it's not the end result, what we feed into our mind is the beginning. ...When our mind lines up with God's Word, eventually our inward belief will line up as well."

JOHN BEVERE
adapted from chapter 15

1. Have you ever asked God to "increase your faith"? The disciples asked Jesus this question, and He answered them, "If you have faith as a *mustard seed*, you can say to this mulberry tree, 'Be pulled up by the roots and be planted in the sea,' and it would obey you" (Luke 17:6).

   a. What was Jesus actually trying to convey to His disciples then and to us now?

   _____

   _____

   _____

   _____

Heaven's APPEAL

Hear instruction and be wise, and do not refuse or neglect it. Blessed (happy, fortunate, to be envied) is the man who listens to me, watching daily at my gates, waiting at the posts of my doors. For whoever finds me [Wisdom] finds life and draws forth and obtains favor from the Lord.

—Proverbs 8:33-35 AMP

EXTRAORDINARY DEVOTIONAL WORKBOOK

b. Getting God's Word into your heart is the major key to increasing your faith. Read Deuteronomy 6:6-9, Romans 10:8,10 and Psalm 119:11 and write what these indispensable truths communicate to you.

_____

_____

_____

_____

FASCINATING FACT: THE MARVELOUS MUSTARD SEED

Jesus uses the **mustard seed** to give us a tangible illustration of His Kingdom as well as the power of faith. Mustard is a well-known plant with tiny seeds that flourishes in the Holy Land. During Jesus' time, the mustard seed was the smallest seed used by farmers in the region, yet it has the ability to *grow rapidly* into the largest of garden plants. In spite of its tiny size, it delivers a strong, pungent flavor. The strength of its growing roots has been known to be powerful enough to crack cement. Although most plants grow to the height of three to five feet, Palestinian mustard trees have been known to grow to a height of 10 to 15 feet or more.[1]

CHECK OUT THE PARABLE OF THE SOWER IN MATTHEW 13:3-23 AND MARK 4:3-20.

2. Planting God's Word in our hearts is what the parable of the sower is all about. The *seed* represents God's Word and our heart is the *soil*. Jesus said, "If you don't understand this story, you won't understand any others" (Mark 4:13 CEV).

a. What is the real focus of this parable: the *seed* or the *soil*? Why is this so important, especially in light of God's will being done on earth?

_____

_____

_____

b. The seed that fell *upon the path* represents the enemy stealing the Word before it has a chance to reach our heart. List some of the major ways Satan tries to steal the Word. (See page 178 in the book.)

_____

_____

Voice of the Ages

"You say, 'How can I increase my faith?' Know more about God. The secret of having more faith is to know more about God. Faith has a direct relationship with our knowledge of God.[2] ...Faith grows and develops in the same ways our physical bodies grow and develop—by eating good food and exercising properly. *The food that faith thrives on is the Word of God* (1 Peter 2:2; Romans 10:17), and the faith in our hearts is to be exercised through regular use."[3]

—Dr. Lester Sumrall

3. The seed that fell on *rocky ground*, sprouted, and then withered represents those who receive the Word joyfully and allow it into their heart, but it doesn't get rooted. Something happens during the **critical belief period** that causes the seed to die.

a. Explain the meaning of *critical belief period*. (See page 179 in the book.)

_____

_____

_____

_____

b. During this time, what can you do to strengthen your faith and ensure that the seed of God's Word gets rooted in your heart and brings forth fruit?

_____

_____

_____

Check out Matthew 14:25-31 for an example of this in Peter's life.

c. Read Psalm 33:18-19; 42:5 and write what these principles speak to your heart.

_____

_____

_____

Have you been greatly distressed? Do as David did (see 1 Samuel 30:6).

"We must remember the **heart** is the *seat of our faith*, where the seed must be planted. This is why we are told, 'Above all else, guard your heart, for it is the wellspring of life' (Proverbs 4:23 NIV). We guard our heart by guarding what enters our mind, for our heart cannot correctly believe unless we are feeding proper knowledge to our mind. ...Correct knowledge in our mind will mean the right information is fed to our heart."

JOHN BEVERE
adapted from session 10

Heaven's APPEAL

[What, what would have become of me] had I not *believed* that I would see the Lord's goodness in the land of the living! Wait and **hope for** and expect the Lord; be brave and of good courage and let your heart be stout and enduring. Yes, wait for and **hope for** and expect the Lord.

—Psalm 27:13-14 AMP

4. The fourth soil Jesus mentions in the parable of the sower is the *good soil*, which produces a bumper crop of 30, 60 or 100 times more than what was sown.

   a. Read Matthew 13:23 and Luke 8:15 and describe the character of the person having a heart of good soil that enables him to produce an extraordinary crop.

   _____

   _____

   _____

   _____

   b. Which of the four soils would you say currently represents your heart? Why?

   _____

   _____

   _____

Voice of the Ages

"Zeal without knowledge is like a mettled (*courageous, determined*) horse without eyes, or like a sword in a madman's hand; and there is no knowledge where there is not the word: for if they reject the word of the Lord, and act not by that, 'What wisdom is in them?' saith the prophet (Jeremiah 8:9; Isaiah 8:20)."

—John Bunyan[4]
[words in parentheses added for clarity]

5. Ironically, it *is* possible to be zealous and sincerely devoted to God, yet be sincerely *wrong* in what we believe in our heart. This is how many Jewish people were in Jesus and Paul's day and how a number of Christians are today.

   a. How does this happen—how do we miss out on true faith and Christ's abundant provision?

   _____

   _____

   _____

   _____

   _____

   _____

Check out Luke 11:52; Romans 10:2-3.

SIFT

The word *sift* used in Luke 22:31 is the Greek word *siniazo*. While it paints an image of "winnowing grain, sifting and shaking it in a sieve," it literally means "an inward agitation to try one's faith to the verge of overthrow."[5] Thankfully in the midst of this, Jesus our awesome Savior, is praying for us that our faith will not fail (see John 17:15-20; Hebrews 7:25).

b. Write out Paul's passionate plea found in Colossians 1:9-10 and *make it your prayer:*

_____

_____

_____

_____

_____

_____

6. Just as Satan desired to *sift* Peter through trials and troubles, he desires to sift you. He is not really afraid of you making a lot of money, enjoying your life, or even going to heaven one day. But there is something that absolutely terrifies him.

   a. What is it that Satan fears most about you growing and maturing in Christ? (See page 185 in the book.) How much of a threat do you think you currently are to him?

   _____

   _____

   b. Read Psalm 34:17,19 and 1 Corinthians 10:13 and write how these promises regarding trials challenge you.

   _____

   _____

   _____

" The Scripture says Satan is subtle and crafty. His strategies appear extremely 'normal,' which make them difficult to discern. His number one goal is to make God's Word appear 'abnormal' and his words 'normal.' It's the message planted in the *heart*, not the mind, that's a threat to his kingdom of darkness. When Jesus says, 'If you have faith as a mustard seed,' He is not talking about the Word of God in our mind but in our *heart*. "

JOHN BEVERE
adapted from chapter 15

7. It's important to realize that when the enemy attacks you, he is ultimately after your heart. However, he can only access it through your mind. Without question, the *mind is where the fight begins.*

a. According to John 8:44, what's the most important thing to remember about the thoughts Satan brings against you?

_____

_____

b. How are the enemy's *impure, negative* and *fearful* images strengthened in your heart?

_____

_____

c. How are God's positive images of *faith, hope* and *love* strengthened?

_____

_____

Heaven's APPEAL

Can all your worries add a single moment to your life? Of course not! And if worry can't do little things like that, what's the use of worrying over bigger things?
—Luke 12:25-26 NLT

8. *Worry, anxiety* and *fear* are some of Satan's greatest tools to drain you of joy and paint a picture of hopelessness on the screen of your heart. Thankfully, your Father has personally promised to provide for you. He doesn't want you to worry about anything. Instead, He wants you to learn to rest and live in peace with Him.

Voice of the Ages

"The greatest burden we have to carry in life is *self*. ...In casting off your burdens, therefore, the first one you must get rid of is yourself. You must hand yourself and all your inward *experiences*, your *temptations*, your *temperament*, your *frames* and *feelings*, all over into the care and keeping of your God, and leave them there. He made you, and therefore He understands you and knows how to manage you, and you must trust Him to do it."
—**Hannah Whitall Smith**[6]

a. Read Jesus' words in Matthew 6:24-34 and Luke 12:22-34. What is the Holy Spirit speaking to you about worry? How does this strengthen your faith?

_____

_____

b. Read Matthew 6:31-33 and 1 Peter 5:7. What can you do on a practical level to put these words into action?

_____

_____

_____

HOPE

A desire of good, accompanied with an expectation of obtaining it; the highest degree of well founded expectation of good, such as a hope founded on God's gracious promises. Hope is different from *wish* or *desire* in that it implies some confidence of obtaining the good desired. Hope therefore always gives pleasure or joy; while wish and desire may produce or be accompanied with pain and anxiety.[7]

Heaven's APPEAL

(*The Lord*) satisfies your mouth [your necessity and desire at your personal age and situation] with good so that your youth, renewed, is like the eagle's [strong, overcoming, soaring]!
—Psalm 103:5 AMP

[italicized words in parentheses added for clarity]

9. One of the main reasons people struggle to have faith is because *they have no hope*. As Proverbs 13:12 declares, "Hope deferred makes the heart sick, but when dreams come true, there is life and joy" (NLT).

a. In a practical way, explain how *hope* differs from *faith* and how the two work together to produce joy, peace and happiness in your life. (See page 183 in the book.)

_____

_____

_____

b. God's Word is full of references on **hope**. Look up these verses and discover some of the wonderful facets of hope:

LOOK UP	ASK YOURSELF...	ANSWER
1 Peter 1:3	As a born-again believer, what have I been birthed into?	
Romans 15:4,13	What are the two main sources of my hope?	

Psalm 62:5-7; 71:5-6; 119:74	Where am I to put my hope?	
1 Corinthians 13:13 Colossians 1:5	What other "ingredients" spring from and work with hope?	
Hebrews 6:19	How does hope affect my soul (my mind, will and emotions)?	
Psalm 33:18; 147:11	How does the Lord respond to my hope?	
Colossians 1:27	What is my only hope of seeing the image of God's glory reproduced in my life?	
Titus 2:13	What is my most blessed hope?	

"The enemy and God are both contending for the **screen of your heart**. This is the spiritual war zone. For whatever fills the screen and is believed, that is what will come forth in our life. The words we *hear* and *heed* on a daily basis will paint pictures on our heart's screen. This is why Jesus says, 'Be careful what you are hearing' (Mark 4:24 AMP)."

JOHN BEVERE
adapted from chapter 15

10. When communicating God's Word, Jesus told stories of *fish* to fishermen, stories of *farming* to farmers, and stories of *business* to businessmen. He did this so people could understand the truth He was sharing and have an image in their heart they could relate to.

a. What type of work are you involved in on a regular basis? With this in mind, how do you think the Lord is most likely to speak truth to you? Or, how does He speak to you most often?

_____

_____

b. Have you ever thought that God was speaking to you but dismissed it as just "being you" because it sounded too simple and familiar? If so, what did you hear?

_____

_____

c. Don't let the enemy fool you into believing you can't hear from God. The truth is *you can*! Read John 10:4,27 and Isaiah 30:21 and write what these promises from your Father speak to your heart.

_____

_____

11. Abram had a disappointing and hope*less* image in his heart regarding the future of his family lineage. This was the result of experiencing decades of barrenness and the knowledge that Sarai was now beyond her ability to have children. But God changed all that by painting a new, positive picture of hope in his heart (see Genesis 15:1-6).

Heaven's APPEAL

"For I know the plans I have for you," declares the Lord, "plans to prosper you and not to harm you, plans to give you **hope** and a *future*."
—Jeremiah 29:11 NIV

a. What image has life's *experiences* and *knowledge* painted on the screen of your heart?

_____

_____

_____

_____

_____

Voice of the Ages

"My Words shall be life unto thee, for My commandments are given for thy health and for any preservation. They will guard thee from folly, and guide thee away from danger.

Hide My commandments in thy **heart**, and make them the law of thy life. Cherish My words, and take not lightly the least of them. I have not given them to bind thee, but to bring thee into the life of greatest joy and truest liberty."
—**Frances J. Roberts**[8]

b. Has God spoken to you about your future and painted a special picture on the screen of your heart? If so, describe it.

_____

_____

_____

If you are in need of a fresh, new image to generate hope in your heart, *get quiet before the Lord* and humbly ask Him to speak to your heart in a way you can clearly understand. Write what He reveals in the "Notes" section of this chapter.

UNVEIL YOUR HERO

As a teenager, he became impassioned to rescue the millions enslaved by human trafficking. He gives his life to an organization to help end the sex slave trade worldwide.

Justice is being served by **Austin**...

the bottom line

The key to living an extraordinary life of faith is getting God's Word deep within your heart, and the way to get it in your heart is by renewing your mind. As you study and meditate regularly on the promises and principles of Scripture, your heart will have the proper knowledge to draw from. The result will be a positive picture of hope painted on the screen of your heart.

Journal Your Journey

"Here's the bottom line: *No faith* means no access to grace and no ability to please God; *little faith* grants little access to grace and little ability to please God; *great faith* gives great abundance of grace and great ability to please God. It all comes down to faith."

JOHN BEVERE
adapted from chapter 15

EYE-OPENERS

Are you seeing some things about faith that you haven't seen before? Has your view on the importance of God's Word reached a new level? Take time to write what the Lord is revealing.

_____

_____

_____

_____

_____

REVOLUTIONARY YOU

Next to feeding your spirit the truth of God's Word is making sure your heart is *pliable* and *prepared* to receive it. What new objectives is the Holy Spirit prompting you to establish?

_____

_____

_____

_____

A Captive AUDIENCE

Voice of the Ages

We are human, but we don't wage war with human plans and methods. We use God's mighty weapons, not mere worldly weapons, to knock down the Devil's strongholds.
—2 Corinthians 10:3-4 NLT

"No faith is required to do the *possible*; actually only a morsel of this atom-powered stuff is needed to do the *impossible*, for a piece as large as a mustard seed will do more than we have ever dreamed of."
—Leonard Ravenhill[9]

If you've been serving God for any length of time, you are well aware that we are in a war. It's not a physical war with people made of flesh and blood—it's a spiritual war with an unseen enemy. The place where the battle rages the greatest is in our mind. Indeed, the "thought life" is the area where we win or lose the fight.

Every moment of the day, our eyes and ears are busily at work receiving countless clips of information—some good, some bad, and many shades in between. But before our mind categorizes this information, we need to analyze it. Second Corinthians 10:5 gives us some very important instructions regarding how we are to handle what's going on in our mind:

Casting down *imaginations*, and every *high thing* that exalteth itself against the knowledge of God, and bringing into captivity every *thought* to the obedience of Christ.

—2 Corinthians 10:5 KJV

From this verse, we see three major things that we must actively guard against: *imaginations*, *thoughts* and "*high things*" (improper knowledge) that exalt themselves against the true knowledge of God's Word. To cast these things down means to willfully throw down, throw away or discard them. In other words, we **reject** any theory, thought, argument or idea that comes into our mind and attempts to arrogantly supersede or replace the truth of Scripture. We then take it *captive*, confining and imprisoning it, by disproving it with the Word.

Ask yourself: *What type of things does the enemy repeatedly bring to my mind in these areas?*

IMAGINATIONS [ungodly mental images of something not present to the senses]

_____

_____

HIGH THINGS [false, improper knowledge, arguments or theories that challenge God's Word]

_____

_____

THOUGHTS [ideas, notions or opinions that cross your mind and are not in line with Scripture]

_____

_____

"The devil tries to invade your life through lies that he plants in your brain. If you don't take your thoughts captive, it will be just a matter of time before the devil starts using those lies to create mental and emotional strongholds for the purpose of keeping you in bondage. But if you take your thoughts captive, then your thoughts cannot take you captive!"

—**Rick Renner**[10]

Satan would love for you to sit back and receive every thought he drops into your head. One of his most effective disguises is pretending to be *you*. He injects thoughts into your mind using phrases like, "I am...," "I feel...," "I want..." and "I think...," and then completes the idea with negative, discouraging, fear-filled, or ungodly words. Can you detect any patterns like this in your thinking? If so, what are they?

_____

_____

These are the areas you need to search and study in Scripture to discover God's invincible seeds of truth you are to plant in your heart.

STRONGHOLDS

The word *stronghold* is from the Greek word *ouhuroma*, one of the oldest words in the New Testament. It was originally used to describe a *fortress* or *castle*. Ancient fortresses had very high and thick impenetrable walls that were made to keep outsiders from coming in. Interestingly, *ouhuroma* is also the same word in the New Testament for a *prison*. So while a fortress is designed to keep outsiders from getting in, a prison is designed to keep the one inside from getting out.

When someone has a stronghold in his mind or emotions, he has a fortress or castle of wrong thinking in his soul. Invisible, impenetrable walls of lies surround him. Like the walls of a fortress, these lies isolate him from others who attempt to break in and help him see the truth. And like the walls of a prison, they hold him captive in the devil's deception.[11]

While some imaginations and thoughts that the enemy hurls at our head are obvious, others are more subtle. In order to be able to discern the devil's devious deceptions, you must spend regular time in God's Word and in His presence. If a repetitive pattern of ungodly thinking is *accepted* and *fed*, a stronghold will be built. The longer you tolerate it and choose not to confront it with the truth of God's Word, the more deeply rooted and controlling the stronghold becomes.

THINK ABOUT WHAT YOU'RE THINKING ABOUT. Begin to monitor your mind's thoughts and imaginations. Ask yourself, "What kind of fruit is being produced by this thought?" If it is producing feelings of stress, anger, fear, worry, depression, lust, and the like, cast it down in the name of Jesus and speak the Word against it.

Are you wondering if something you are thinking is from God or not? *Meditate on the message* of James 3:17 and describe what true godly wisdom from above sounds like.

_____

_____

_____

After reading about John's battle with sexual perversity, how has your hope and faith been strengthened? What principles can you learn and apply in your own life?

_____

_____

_____

Voice of the Ages

"The condition your mind should be in is described in [Philippians 4:8]. You have the mind of Christ; begin to use it. If He wouldn't think it, you shouldn't either. It is by this continual 'watching over' your thoughts that you begin to take every thought captive unto the obedience of Jesus Christ (see 2 Corinthians 10:5 KJV).

The Holy Spirit is quick to remind you if your mind is beginning to take you in a wrong direction, then the decision becomes yours. Will you flow in the mind of the flesh or in the mind of the Spirit? One leads to death, the other to life. The choice is yours. Choose life!"

—Joyce Meyer[12]
[words in brackets added for clarity]

Remember, you must think right, godly thoughts *on purpose*—they're not just going to fall on you. Effort is required. Write out Philippians 4:8, making it a model for your mind to live by.

_____

_____

_____

_____ Philippians 4:8

Prayer of Dedication

Lord, thank You for this eye-opening study. I ask You to tear down any stronghold of wrong thinking in my mind. By Your grace, help me develop the habit of casting down and taking captive every ungodly thought and imagination that comes into my mind. I'm hungry for You and Your Word. Help me establish the discipline I need to daily feed my spirit. Break up any hard, infertile soil in my heart. I want to be pliable and receptive to Your truth. As I do my part and study, I ask You to give me total recall of Your Word, chapter and verse. If the enemy can bring back to my mind ungodly images from movies and profane lyrics from songs I've heard in the past, then surely You are more than able to give me total recall of Your Word. Thank You for loving me and answering my prayer...in Jesus' name, Amen!

FOR FURTHER STUDY

THE HEALTHY HEART
Deuteronomy 11:18-20
Psalm 40:8; 51:10-12; 73:25-26
Proverbs 12:25; 17:22
Ezekiel 11:19; 36:26
Hebrews 10:22-23

THE POWER OF HIS WORD
Psalm 107:20
Isaiah 55:10-11
Jeremiah 23:29

LOOKING & LISTENING TO GOD
Proverbs 18:15
Isaiah 50:4-5
Luke 10:38-42
John 10:4,16,27
Revelation 3:20

John 17:17; Ephesians 5:26
Hebrews 4:12

NOTES

_____

1. Adapted from *The New Unger's Bible Dictionary*, Merrill F. Unger (Chicago, IL: Moody Press, 1988) p. 1335; and *Information on a Mustard Seed* (http://en.wikipedia.org/wiki/Mustard_seed, retrieved 6/10/09). 2. Dr. Lester Sumrall, *Faith Can Change Your World* (South Bend, IN: Sumrall Publishing, 1999) p. 78. 3. Ibid., p. 39. 4. Quotes by John Bunyan (http://dailychristianquote.com/dcqbunyan.html, retrieved 6/22/09). 5. *Thayer's Greek English Lexicon of the New Testament*, Joseph H. Thayer (Grand Rapids, MI: Baker Book House Company, 1977) p. 576. 6. Hannah Whitall Smith, *The Christian's Secret of a Happy Life* (Gainesville, FL: Bridge-Logos, 1998) p. 22. 7. *Noah Webster's First Edition of an American Dictionary of the English Language* (1828), Republished in facsimile edition by Foundation for American Christian Education (San Francisco, CA 1995). 8. Frances J. Roberts, *Come Away My Beloved* (Ojai, CA: King's Farspan, Inc., 1973) p. 22. 9. Quotes by Leonard Ravenhill (http://dailychristianquote.com/dcqravenhill.html, retrieved 6/22/09). 10. Rick Renner, *Sparkling Gems from the Greek* (Tulsa, OK: Teach All Nations, 2003) p. 370. 11. Ibid., adapted from pp. 918-919. 12. Joyce Meyer, *Battlefield of the Mind* (New York, NY: FaithWords, 2002) p. 181.

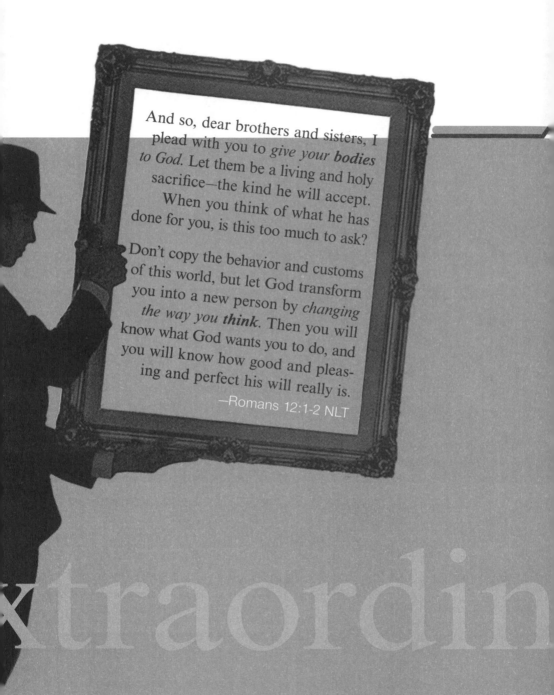

And so, dear brothers and sisters, I plead with you to *give your bodies to God*. Let them be a living and holy sacrifice—the kind he will accept. When you think of what he has done for you, is this too much to ask?

Don't copy the behavior and customs of this world, but let God transform you into a new person by *changing the way you think*. Then you will know what God wants you to do, and you will know how good and pleasing and perfect his will really is.

—Romans 12:1-2 NLT

The Flesh

Please refer to chapter 16 in the *Extraordinary* book, along with session 11 of the teaching series.

THE FLESH

> In virtually every occurrence, the word *flesh* used in the New Testament is taken from the Greek word *sarx*... and generally refers to the **body** (as opposed to the soul or spirit); it's the symbol of what is *external*.[1]

1. Out of all the things God created, man holds a position like no other. Genesis 1:27 declares that we were created *in the image of God*, and just as He is three in one, we are three in one—*body*, *soul* and *spirit*.

    a. Take a moment to stop and think about the fact that you've been created in the very likeness of God. Do you really believe this? How do your thoughts, words and actions prove that?

    _____

    _____

    _____

    b. Briefly describe the *function* of the spirit, soul and body and their relationship to each other.

    _____

    _____

    _____

    c. When it comes to our spirit, soul and body, what is the major difference between an *unsaved* person and a saved person? (See page 197 in the book.)

    _____

    _____

    _____

Check out Ephesians 2:1-6.

2. In light of all we've learned, it's important to understand how the **heart** fits into the overall picture. Read Hebrews 4:12 and explain the location and makeup of your heart. What is the only thing that can help you properly understand your heart's motives?

_____

_____

_____

_____

Voice of the Ages

"Christ's purpose for the world was that man, like Himself, should become the dwelling place of God. It was purposed that mankind should be as holy and desirable a dwelling place of God as was Jesus Himself.[2] ...God lives in a man's *spirit*, the spirit of man reaching out into the boundless, touching the almightiness of God, discerning His nature, appropriating His power, securing His almightiness. God lives in a man's *flesh*, giving off a vibration of God-life, God-power, God indwelling in his blood, God indwelling in his hands, God indwelling his bones and marrow—a habitation of God."[3]

—John G. Lake

Heaven's APPEAL

Jesus answered, If a person [really] loves Me, he will keep My word [obey My teaching]; and My Father will love him, and We will come to him and make Our home (abode, *special dwelling place*) with him.

—John 14:23 AMP

3. God desires you to experience *complete* salvation—spirit, soul and body. When Jesus died and rose again, He secured this privilege for every man and woman who puts their faith in Him. Briefly explain *how* and *when* each part of your being is saved. (See page 199 in the book.)

MY **SPIRIT** BEING SAVED: *JUSTIFICATION*

_____

_____

_____

_____

_____

_____

_____

Check out John 3:3-6; 2 Corinthians 5:17.

MY **SOUL** BEING SAVED: *SANCTIFICATION*

_____

_____

_____

Check out James 1:21; Philippians 2:12-13; John 17:17.

MY **BODY** BEING SAVED: *GLORIFICATION*

_____

_____

_____

Check out 1 Corinthians 15:35-44; 2 Corinthians 5:1-3; Philippians 3:20-21.

161

"It's obvious our present body is not redeemed but still corruptible. However, we're no longer slaves to appetites, lusts, pride, selfishness, and other traits of fallen flesh, unless we *choose* to be. We can now draw upon the strength of our new nature and live by it rather than by the flesh. The determining factor is our *soul*, for it's the **decision maker**."

JOHN BEVERE
adapted from chapter 16

4. One day you will have a glorified body just like Jesus! For a preview, read these passages that talk about Jesus *after* He was raised from the dead. Look for both His *natural* and *supernatural* physical traits and senses and jot them down.

JESUS' BODY	IN YOUR GLORIFIED BODY, YOU WILL HAVE AND BE ABLE TO...
Matthew 28:9-10; Luke 24:36-40	
Luke 24:41-43 John 21:10-13	
John 20:16-17	
John 21:1-14	
John 20:19-20,26-27 Luke 24:30-31	

You can **check out** the full story of Jesus' interaction with His followers after His resurrection in Luke 24:13-53 and John 20:11-31; 21 and Acts 1:1-9.

5. Sadly, many Christians mistakenly credit their flesh with the dominating upper hand in their life, and because they *believe* their fleshly desires are hard to resist, they largely live under its control. It all comes back to *faith*—what you believe is what you get.

    a. From where does your *flesh* get its input and direction, and how does it gather it? What about your *spirit*—from where does it receive its influence?

    _____

    _____

    _____

    b. What is meant by your soul being the *decision maker*? How does it determine the progress of your sanctification?

    _____

    _____

    _____

Heaven's APPEAL

So get rid of all uncleanness and the rampant outgrowth of wickedness, and in a humble (gentle, modest) spirit receive and welcome the Word which *implanted* and *rooted* [in your hearts] contains the power to save your **souls**. But be doers of the Word [obey the message], and not merely listeners to it, betraying yourselves [into deception by reasoning contrary to the Truth].

—James 1:21-22 AMP

c. Is there any area of your life lacking self-control because you've put the blame on your flesh, thus living under its dominance? If so, what is that area and how is God calling you to action?

_____

_____

_____

_____

_____

_____

_____

> **"** Our **soul** is the only part of our being in which we determine the *rate* of salvation. We cooperate by *hearing*, *believing* and *obeying*, which in turn speeds up the process or, conversely, slows it down. The transformation of our soul is crucial to extraordinary living on earth, along with finishing well as believers. **"**

JOHN BEVERE
adapted from chapter 16

6. *Oneness* with the Father was a recurring theme in Jesus' teaching. He said, "I and My Father are *one*," "...the Father is in Me, and I in Him," "...the Father who dwells in Me does the works," and "...the Son can do nothing of Himself..." (John 10:30,38; 14:10; 5:19).

 a. Read 1 Corinthians 6:17-20 and Job 32:8 and write what these passages concerning the significance of your spirit mean to you:

_____

_____

_____

Heaven's APPEAL

Therefore, [there is] now no condemnation (no adjudging guilty of wrong) for those who are *in Christ Jesus*, who live [and] walk not after the dictates of the flesh, but after the dictates of the Spirit. For the **law of the Spirit of life** [which is] in Christ Jesus [the law of our new being] has freed me from the *law of sin and of death*.
—Romans 8:1-2 AMP

Voice of the Ages

"All the dealings of God with the soul of the believer are in order to bring him into *oneness* with Himself, that the prayer of our Lord may be fulfilled... Oneness with Christ must, in the very nature of things, consist in a Christ-like life and character. It is not what we feel, but what we are that settles the question. No matter how exalted or intense our emotions on the subject may be, if there is not a likeness of character with Christ, a unity of aim and purpose, a similarity of thought and of action, there can be no real oneness."

—Hannah Whitall Smith[4]

7. Through repentance of sin and faith in Christ's completed work, you are *born again*. You are placed *in Christ* and are a new creation altogether. This means you are set free from the law of sin and death and are now under a new law—*the law of the Spirit of life*.

 a. Using the practical example of the law of gravity and Daniel Bernoulli's law of lift, explain how the law of the Spirit of life sets you free from the law of sin and death.

_____

_____

b. Does the law of the Spirit of life do away with the law of sin and death? Can you as a believer be placed back under the control of the law of sin and death? If so, how?

_____

_____

_____

c. Have you been living more under the law of the Spirit of life, or the law of sin and death? How do your thoughts, words and actions prove that?

_____

_____

_____

8. *Meditate on the message* of these passages regarding what it means to live according to the flesh and the Spirit:

> For those who live according to the flesh set their minds on the things of the flesh, but those who live according to the Spirit, (set their minds on) the things of the Spirit. For to be carnally (fleshly) minded is death, but to be spiritually minded is life and peace.
>
> **—Romans 8:5-6 NKJV**
> [words in parentheses added for clarity]

> And set your minds and keep them set on what is above (the higher things), not on the things that are on the earth. For [as far as this world is concerned] you have died, and your [new, real] life is hidden with Christ in God.
>
> **—Colossians 3:2-3 AMP**

a. What is the Holy Spirit showing you about living according to the flesh?

_____

_____

_____

b. What is He revealing to you about living according to the Spirit?

_____

_____

_____

c. According to Romans 8:5-8, why are so many in the church living the same as those in the world? Do you find yourself in this position? If so, what must you do?

_____

_____

_____

Heaven's APPEAL

Those who look to him are *radiant*; their faces are never covered with shame.

—Psalm 34:5 NIV

9. The sobering truth is that the mind of the flesh is death and if we live according to the flesh we will die (see Romans 8:6,13). Therefore, in order to stay as far away from death as possible, it is imperative that we learn to live by the Spirit.

a. Explain the two-fold remedy to keep you from gravitating toward following the flesh.

_____

_____

_____

_____

_____

Check out Galatians 5:16.

Voice of the Ages

"Our flesh is purged by the divine power being transmitted from our spirit through our soul into our body.

When we contemplate the Lord Jesus on the Mount of Transfiguration and think of the *radiant glory* that came through His *flesh*, not just the illumination of His Spirit, but the holy glory emanating through His flesh until He became white and glistening, until His face shone as the light, we begin to understand the transfiguring power of heaven.

It is that radiant purity of God that my soul covets. It is that *radiant power*, evidenced in the pureness of my spirit, my mind, and my very *flesh* that I long for."

—**John G. Lake**[5]

b. Read Romans 8:10-13. What is the Holy Spirit revealing to you in these verses about His power working in your *physical body*?

_____

_____

_____

Heaven's APPEAL

God's Spirit beckons. There are things to do and places to go! This resurrection life you received from God is *not* a timid, grave-tending life. It's adventurously expectant, greeting God with a childlike "What's next, Papa?"
—Romans 8:14-15 The Message

" Life in Christ is *adventurous, exciting* and *expectant.* In a word—**extraordinary**! We are now free from the law of sin and death that once enslaved us. We no longer have to follow fallen flesh's desires. Our *spirit* along with our *body* has been affected by our new life in Christ. What an amazing salvation! *"*

JOHN BEVERE
adapted from chapter 16

10. God's Word declares that Jesus has set us free to live a life of freedom, but in order to *stay* free, we must take a stand spiritually and not be enslaved again by our sinful flesh or legalism (see Galatians 5:1). Clearly, we're not to use our freedom as a license to live carelessly.

a. According to Galatians 5:13-14, for what are you to use your freedom?

_____

b. Have you ever fallen back into ungodly behavior you were once free from? What was it that re-ensnared you, and how did you get free?

_____

_____

Heaven's APPEAL

Do not let any part of your body become a tool of wickedness, to be used for sinning. Instead, give yourselves completely to God since you have been given new life. And *use your whole body* as a tool to do what is right for the glory of God.
—Romans 6:13 NLT

FASCINATING FACT: THE FABULOUS FIVE

Our *five senses* give us some astonishing capabilities. We can see a candle's flame 30 miles away on a dark, clear night, and smell a single drop of perfume diffused in a three-room apartment. We can taste .04 ounces of table salt in 530 quarts of water. Our sense of touch can detect a pressure that depresses the skin .00004 inches on the face or fingertips. And we can tell where a sound is coming from even when it arrives at one ear just .0003 seconds before its arrival at the other ear.[6] Take these amazing abilities, surrender them to the Spirit that raised Christ from the dead living in you, and watch what He does!

11. In order to maintain true freedom in Christ and receive His grace, we must daily present our body to Him as a *living sacrifice* and cooperate with His Holy Spirit to *totally renew our mind.* In your own words, explain what these life-giving habits mean:

TO *GIVE MY BODY TO GOD* AS A LIVING SACRIFICE MEANS...

_____

_____

ALLOWING GOD TO *TOTALLY RENEW MY MIND* MEANS...

_____

_____

" I've learned through experience that when I read the Bible with a clear mind and heart, it opens up the channel of my spirit's influence to my soul. It's as if the passageway from my spirit to my soul is cleared so I can hear the instruction of the Holy Spirit. I've discovered that I see clearer, think better, and my body seems to have more life and empowerment. If I *don't* hear the Word of God, then it seems as if the influence of the world creeps in and I find myself conforming more to the customs and ways of this world. "

JOHN BEVERE
adapted from chapter 16

12. The importance of feeding on God's Word regularly cannot be stressed enough. Indeed, the truth of Scripture is the *power of God to bring salvation* to every area of your life (see Romans 1:16). *Get quiet before the Lord.* Ask Him to show you a creative plan for getting the Word into your mind and heart while you're at home, in your car, at work and everywhere you go.

_____

_____

_____

_____

Voice of the Ages

"The Spirit-filled walk demands...that we live in the Word of God as a fish lives in the sea. By this I do *not* mean that we study the Bible merely, nor that we take a 'course' in Bible doctrine. I mean that we should 'meditate day and night' in the sacred Word, that we should love it and feast upon it and digest it every hour of the day and night. When the business of life compels our attention, we may yet, by a kind of blessed mental reflex, keep the Word of Truth ever before our minds."

—A.W. Tozer[7]

UNVEIL YOUR HERO

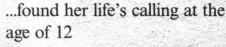

...found her life's calling at the age of 12

—Mother Theresa

the bottom line

Jesus Christ has completely paid for our freedom. Through faith in Him, we have grace to live extraordinarily. But in order to remain in His grace and not give in to the desires of our flesh, we must live in the Spirit—giving our bodies to the Lord as a living sacrifice and allowing Him to live through us and totally transform our thinking.

Journal Your Journey

> ...everything—and I do mean everything—connected with that old way of life has to go. It's rotten through and through. Get rid of it! And then take on an entirely new way of life—a God-fashioned life, a life renewed from the inside and working itself into your conduct as God accurately reproduces his character in you.
> —Ephesians 4:22-24 The Message

EYE-OPENERS
Proverbs 29:18 says that when we attend to what God reveals, we are most *blessed* (The Message). What new understanding is God revealing about the connection between your spirit, soul and body?

REVOLUTIONARY YOU
Is the Lord asking you to make any adjustments? Write out any new goals He's asking you to set in order to more consistently walk in the Spirit and not gratify the cravings of your flesh.

Prayer of Dedication

Father, please forgive me for living my life according to the flesh. I repent and humbly ask for Your grace to change. Help me focus on and live according to Your Spirit. Give me the strength and desire to honor You at all times in my body, the temple of Your Holy Spirit. I surrender my life to You as a living sacrifice, desiring to die daily to my fleshly desires (see 1 Corinthians 15:31). *Help me cooperate with You and see my mind renewed by Your Word...in Jesus' name, Amen!*

The Power of
BEING PROACTIVE

> **Keep your eyes on Jesus,** who both began and finished this race we're in. Study how he did it. Because he never lost sight of where he was headed—that exhilarating finish in and with God—he could put up with anything along the way: cross, shame, whatever. And now he's there, in the place of honor, right alongside God.
> —Hebrews 12:2 The Message

I think you'll agree that any believer who has a true heart after God wants to please Him. Those devoted to the Father deeply desire to crucify their flesh and live daily in the Spirit. The question is: *how do we do it?* The answer is: by being *proactive*. In other words, **FOCUS** on the positive image of what we want to be, instead of the negative image of what we're trying to avoid.

As a believer, there's no greater image to set your gaze upon than Jesus. Although you can't see Him physically, you can look intently at Him in the pages of Scripture, studying how He lived.

FOCUS

To concentrate attention or energy; a center of interest or activity. To focus creates a condition in which something can be clearly apprehended or perceived; the state of maximum distinctness or clarity of an image.[8] Interestingly, the original Latin root word for "focus" is a *hearth of fire*. When we focus on Jesus, an unquenchable *fire* of passion for Him is set ablaze!

A.W. Tozer, treasured author of more than 40 books and seasoned pastor of more than 30 years, had some keen insights concerning where our eyes need to be...

...We are instructed to run life's race 'looking unto Jesus, the author and finisher of our faith' (Hebrews 12:2). From all this we learn that *faith* is not a once-done act, but **a continuous gaze of the heart** at the Triune God.

Believing, then, is directing the heart's attention to Jesus. It is lifting the mind to 'Behold the Lamb of God' (John 1:29), and never ceasing that beholding for the rest of our lives. ...Distractions may hinder, but once the heart is committed to Him, after each brief excursion away from Him, the attention will return again and rest upon Him like a wandering bird coming back to its window.

...The man who has struggled to purify himself and has had nothing but repeated failures will experience *real relief* when he stops tinkering with his soul and looks away to the perfect One. While he looks at Christ, the very things he has so long been trying to do will be getting done within him. It will be God working in him to will and to do.

Faith is not in itself a meritorious act; the merit is in the One toward Whom it is directed. Faith is a redirecting of our sight, a getting out of the focus of our own vision and getting God into focus.[9]

The proactive approach of fixing our eyes on Jesus means we are positive, upbeat and living life in a forward, purposeful direction. The opposite approach is to be *reactive* or *passive*. That is, instead of moving forward by faith, we sit still in neutral trying to hold our own, or even worse, we live life in reverse focused on all our failures and the negative things going on around us.

What is the Holy Spirit showing you through A.W. Tozer's excerpt?

_____

_____

How would you describe the way you live the majority of the time—*proactive* or *reactive*? Why?

_____

_____

If we live our Christian life in a reactive mode, we become *defensive* and tend to have a legalistic or religious outlook. What does a person with this view tend to focus on? According to 1 Corinthians 15:56, what does trying to follow a list of rules and regulations end up causing?

_____

_____

Name some practical ways you can **set your mind** on the things of the Spirit.

_____

_____

WHERE YOUR ATTENTION GOES, THE POWER FLOWS!

Indeed, what you focus on grows stronger. That being said, take the next week to meditate on these principles from God's Word. Read them *out loud* once in the morning before you start your day and once at night before you go to bed. Don't rush through them; take your time and focus on what you are saying. At the end of the week, journal any changes you notice in your attitude, thoughts, speech and actions.

MEDITATE on these PERSONALIZED PRINCIPLES

I am the righteousness of God through Jesus Christ my Savior and Lord.

—2 Corinthians 5:21

I have been crucified with Christ and I no longer live, but Christ lives in me. The life I live in the body, I live by faith in the Son of God, who loved me and gave himself for me. I do not set aside the grace of God.

—Galatians 2:20-21 NIV

I think of and see myself as dead to sin—my relation to it completely broken. But I am alive to God, living in unbroken fellowship with Him. Sin no longer dominates and controls me since I am not under the law but under grace.

—Romans 6:11,14 AMP

I walk and live habitually in the Holy Spirit; I am responsive to and controlled by the Spirit. I do not gratify the cravings and desires of my flesh.

—Galatians 5:16 AMP

I am in Jesus Christ and I am not condemned because I follow the direction of the Holy Spirit, not the commands of my flesh. I am free from the law of sin and death and under the law of the Spirit of life.

—Romans 8:1-2 AMP

I walk by faith in God and His Word; I don't walk by what I see or hear in the natural.

—2 Corinthians 5:7 NKJV

I do all things without grumbling, faultfinding and complaining against God and questioning and doubting myself and others.
—Philippians 2:14 AMP

I have the love of God and walk in the love of God. I am patient and kind, not envious, proud, rude, or self-centered. I am not easily angered and I do not keep a record of the wrong things others do. I hate evil and rejoice in the truth, always protecting, always trusting, always hoping, always persevering. God's love in me never fails
—1 Corinthians 13:4-8 NIV

I have strength to do all things and am ready for anything through Jesus Christ who infuses me with inner strength.
—Philippians 4:13 AMP

[note: these personalized verses are not the exact quote from scripture]

Date Started: _____

Speaking the proactive principles of God's Word over my life produced...

_____

_____

_____

_____

_____

Date Completed: _____

Are there other scriptures you would like to see "fleshed out" in your life? Write them in a personalized format and begin confessing them out loud over your life every day. Watch what happens!

FOR FURTHER STUDY

GOD'S SPIRIT LIVES IN YOU!
  Romans 8:9
  1 Corinthians 3:16
  2 Corinthians 6:16
  Ephesians 2:22; 3:17-19

GOD'S POWER TRANSFORMS YOU
  Philippians 1:6; 2:12-13
  1 Thessalonians 5:23-24
  Titus 3:5
  Hebrews 13:20-21

SUBDUE YOUR FLESH
  Romans 13:13-14
  1 Corinthians 9:27

  Galatians 5:24-25
  1 Peter 2:11; 4:1-2

NOTES

1. James L. Strong, LL.D., S.T.D, *Strong's Exhaustive Concordance of the Bible* (Nashville, TN: Thomas Nelson Publishers, 1990), adapted. 2. John G. Lake, *Spiritual Hunger, The God-Men and Other Sermons* (Dallas, TX: Christ for the Nations, Inc., 1979) p. 95. 3. Ibid., p. 103. 4. Hannah Whitall Smith, *The Christian's Secret of a Happy Life* (Gainesville, FL: Bridge-Logos, 1998) pp. 187-189. 5. See note 2, p. 47. 6. Illustrations on the *Flesh* (http://bible.org/illus. php?topic_id=177, retrieved 6/24/09). 7. A.W. Tozer, *A Treasury of A.W. Tozer* (Harrisburg, PA: Christian Publications, Inc., 1980) p. 80. 8. Definition of *Focus* (http://www.answers.com/ topic/focal-point, retrieved 6/26/09). 9. A.W. Tozer, *The Pursuit of God* (Camp Hill, PA: Christian Publications, 1993) pp. 84-85.

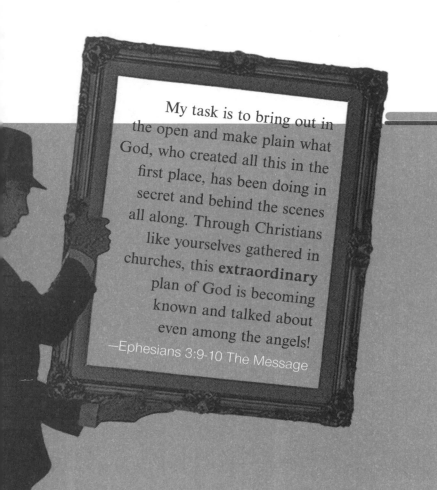

My task is to bring out in the open and make plain what God, who created all this in the first place, has been doing in secret and behind the scenes all along. Through Christians like yourselves gathered in churches, this **extraordinary** plan of God is becoming known and talked about even among the angels!

—Ephesians 3:9-10 The Message

God's Imperial Rule

12

12

Please refer to chapter 17 in the *Extraordinary* book,
along with session 12 of the teaching series.

> **When** Jesus speaks of the Kingdom of God, He's actually referring to the 'rule of God.' The Greek words most frequently used in the gospels for the Kingdom of God are *basileia tou Theos*. *Theos* refers to God, while *basileia* is defined as 'royalty, rule, or reign.' Some scholars believe the best translation for the Kingdom of God is **'God's Imperial Rule'** or 'God's domain.' So Jesus literally communicates, 'Our Father in heaven, God Almighty, Your *Imperial Rule* come, Your will be done on earth just as it is in heaven.' **"**

JOHN BEVERE
adapted from chapter 17

MPERIAL

The word *imperial* "pertains to an empire or royalty; it denotes sovereignty as well as commanding and maintaining supremacy."[1] Words synonymous with *imperial* are grand, regal, majestic, and royal.

1. Adam messed up in the Garden of Eden and gave Satan dominion over the earth. However, Jesus, as a man, won it back. Now final authority is back where God originally intended—in the hands of *His* men and women.

    a. Why has God limited Himself in what He'll do on earth? (See page 218 in the book.)

    _____

    _____

    b. Who ultimately determines whether or not the will of God is done on the earth? What does this say to you personally?

    _____

    _____

    _____

2. According to Amos 3:7, God revealed His will to His servants (the prophets) in the days of the Old Testament. Today, in the era of the New Testament, He reveals His will to believers. What is God's purpose in revealing His will to us—what does He want us to do?

_____

_____

_____

Check out John 15:15; 16:13.

Heaven's APPEAL

The heaven of heavens is for God, but he put us in charge of the earth.
— Psalm 115:16 The Message

QUICK REVIEW
SHOW WHAT YOU KNOW

What is your highest goal as a believer?

_____

_____

According to 2 Peter 1:3, how are you to carry out this goal?

_____

_____

_____

Name three specific things that God's amazing grace provides for you.

_____

_____

_____

Where does faith *originate*, and how does it enable you to receive God's grace?

_____

_____

_____

_____

Name the primary way in which you can *increase your faith*. (See page 176 in the book.)

_____

_____

_____

3. It's important for you to have a clear understanding of the Kingdom of God (God's Imperial Rule). **Check out** Jesus' practical descriptions in these passages and allow the Holy Spirit to paint a fresh, vivid picture of His Kingdom on the screen of your heart.

SCRIPTURE	JESUS COMPARES HIS KINGDOM/IMPERIAL RULE TO:	WHAT DOES THIS SIGNIFY OR IMPLY?
Matthew 13:24-30	Sowing weeds among good seed	
Matthew 13:33 Luke 13:20-21	The effects of yeast	
Matthew 13:44	Hidden treasure in a field	
Matthew 13:45-46	A merchant looking for pearls	
Matthew 13:47-50	A fisherman's net; separating the good fish from the bad	
Matthew 22:2-14	The wedding banquet	
Mark 4:26-29	A man sowing seed/ growing seed	
Luke 13:18-19 Mark 4:30-32 Matthew 13:31-32	A mustard seed	

Heaven's APPEAL

...those who receive God's abundant provision of grace and of the gift of righteousness **reign in life** through the one man, Jesus Christ.

—Romans 5:17 NIV

Voice of the Ages

"Do all the good you can. By all the means you can. In all the ways you can. In all the places you can. At all the times you can. To all the people you can. As long as ever you can."

—**John Wesley**[2]

4. When Jesus walked the earth, He gave us an example of how to rule and reign in life. Before He ascended back to heaven, He commissioned all of His followers, including us, to do the same, continuing the work He began.

a. In your own words, describe what it means to rule in life. What kind of things should be happening in your sphere of influence as you live this lifestyle?

_____

_____

_____

b. Give an example of how your extraordinary living is affecting others around you.

_____

_____

_____

Heaven's APPEAL

Each person is given something to do that shows who God is: Everyone gets in on it, everyone benefits.

—1 Corinthians 12:7
The Message

FASCINATING FACTS: DID YOU KNOW...

Johannes Gutenberg *invented the movable type printing press* in 1454, revolutionizing the world. The first book to be printed was the Bible. Gutenberg's superior invention opened the door for the common man to own and know God's Word. The reason for Gutenberg's success, as he stated in 1460, is that his work had been under "the protection of the All-Highest, who often reveals to the humble what He conceals from the wise."

Isaac Newton was just an average student whose best grades were in religion. Nonetheless, his discoveries in physics, optics, astronomy and mathematics place him as the greatest scientific mind of all time. His *formulation of the law of gravity* was his highest achievement and came from his intense study of the Bible. In his words, "I find more sure marks of authenticity in the Bible than in any profane history whatsoever."

Florence Nightingale was convinced at age 17 that God had a special mission planned for her, which she eventually discovered was nursing. Mastering five languages and intensely studying medicine, hospital administration and nursing, Florence became an expert on public health and hospitals, in time overseeing the welfare of the British army. When soldiers tried to give honor to her, she would tell them, "Give praise to God." Indeed, Florence impacted history by *establishing nursing as a medical profession.*

George Washington Carver was the son of a slave woman who became an orphan raised by a poor family. After overcoming serious illness as a child, Carver invested his life in helping others. Describing himself as a "cook-stove chemist," George *developed 300 products from peanuts*, including dyes, soap, and dairy substitutes. He also *formulated more than 100 products from sweet potatoes*, such as molasses and rubber. Who did he give the credit to? God. He explained, "I love to think of nature as an unlimited broadcasting system through which God speaks to us every hour, if we will only tune in."[3]

These people were all *ordinary* Christians who lived *extraordinary* lives in their field of expertise, doing what God called them to do.
WHAT LASTING LEGACY ARE **YOU** LEAVING?

5. Clearly, you have a specific assignment from God. No task, no matter how menial it may seem, is insignificant. Every part is important to the overall function of God's plan—*including yours*!

   a. To the best of your knowledge, what do you feel in your heart God has called you to do in this season of your life? Are you doing it? If not, why?

   _____

   _____

   _____

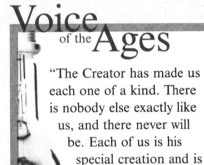

Voice of the Ages

"The Creator has made us each one of a kind. There is nobody else exactly like us, and there never will be. Each of us is his special creation and is alive for a distinctive purpose."
—Luci Swindoll[4]

   b. What should your attitude be toward your task? Read Colossians 3:23-24 and write what this verse of instruction speaks to you.

   _____

   _____

   _____

   _____

c. How are you to use your time? Read Psalm 90:12 and Ephesians 5:15-17 and write what these words of wisdom convey to you.

_____

_____

_____

Who shall separate us from the love of Christ? Shall tribulation, or distress, or persecution, or famine, or nakedness, or peril, or sword? Yet in all these things we are more than conquerors through Him who loved us.

—Romans 8:35,37 NKJV

6. Many believers view trials and tribulation as a major roadblock to living an extraordinary life, but God doesn't want us to see things that way. He wants us to view adversity as major *opportunities* to manifest and advance His Kingdom in and through our lives.

a. What has been your view of opposition and hardship until now? How do you think it has affected your circumstances?

_____

_____

b. Read John 16:33, 2 Corinthians 12:9-10 and James 1:2-3 and write how your perspective of trials is challenged and/or encouraged.

_____

_____

_____

c. Looking back over your life, can you see a time of trouble you went through that actually served to prepare you to rule and reign in life at a later time? If so, explain it.

_____

_____

_____

"I have a dream of a **light-filled** body of Christ comprised of all ages, inclusive of men and women, awakening to what God has hidden within and arising in His glory and power. These believers will live in such an extraordinary manner that multitudes will be drawn to the Kingdom of God, not merely by what they preach, but by the compelling demonstration of how they live and their remarkable feats."

JOHN BEVERE
adapted from chapter 17

7. God doesn't expect us to take over the world and present it to His Son when He returns, but He does expect us to faithfully occupy until He comes.

   a. As a believer, what are some of the things you should be doing as you await Christ's return? **Check out** these verses for the answer:

   Matthew 24:42-51; 25:1-13 • 1 Thessalonians 5:1-5

   _____

   _____

   _____

Heaven's APPEAL

All of us must quickly carry out the tasks assigned us by the one who sent me, because there is little time left before the night falls and all work comes to an end.

—John 9:4 NLT

8. One day the man of ultimate evil, the antichrist, will arise and take center stage on the earth. But before he can, there is something that must be removed—something that is presently concealing and restraining him from being seen and known by all.

   a. What is restraining and concealing the antichrist, and how and when will it be removed? (See page 222 in the book.)

   _____

   _____

   _____

   _____

Voice of the Ages

"Rise up, then, and lay claim to the power that is yours, because I am in you, and ye are in Me, and as I was in the world, even so are ye. I was victorious, and you too may be victorious. I withstood every encounter with the devil, and you too can stand against him. I healed the sick and wrestled tortured bodies out of the grip of evil forces, and you too can do the same. **Learn to reign**, for lo, I have made you to become kings and priests. I have purposed that ye should come into that place where ye share My authority and thus I will be able to manifest forth My glory through you."

—Frances J. Roberts[5]

Check out 2 Thessalonians 2:1-7; 1 Thessalonians 4:16-17.

b. According to 2 Thessalonians 2:1-7, what else is being restrained from being released in the earth?

_____

_____

_____

9. In Scripture, the church is often called the body of Christ, but it is also referred to as the *Bride of Christ*. Read 2 Corinthians 11:2 and Revelation 19:6-8 and 21:2 and give a brief description of the condition of the Bride of Christ before Jesus, the Groom, returns. As part of His Bride, why is this important for you to know?

_____

_____

_____

_____

Heaven's APPEAL

If I speak with human eloquence and angelic ecstasy but don't love, I'm nothing but the creaking of a rusty gate. If I speak God's Word with power, revealing all his mysteries and making everything plain as day, and if I have faith that says to a mountain, 'Jump,' and it jumps, but I don't love, I'm nothing. If I give everything I own to the poor and even go to the stake to be burned as a martyr, but I don't love, I've gotten nowhere. So, no matter what I say, what I believe, and what I do, I'm bankrupt without love.

—1 Corinthians 13:1-3
The Message

10. If there is any quality a groom wants his bride to have, it's *love*, and Jesus wants this for His Bride too. We can know the entire Bible from cover to cover and walk in the power of God 24/7, but if we don't embody the genuine love of the Lord, we're nothing.

a. How do we *receive* the ability to love others like God loves us, and how does that love grow? *Meditate on the message* of these amazing truths for the answer:

Romans 5:5 • Ephesians 3:16-19 • 1 John 4:16-19

_____

_____

_____

b. What does love *think*, *speak* and *act* like? Read 1 Corinthians 13:4-8 and write what the picture speaks to you.

_____

_____

_____

_____

_____

_____

_____

_____

_____

_____

Heaven's APPEAL

And so faith, hope, love abide [faith—conviction and belief respecting man's relation to God and divine things; hope—joyful and confident expectation of eternal salvation; love—true affection for God and man, growing out of God's love for and in us], these three; but the *greatest* of these is **love**.

—1 Corinthians 13:13 AMP

the bottom line

You were created to live an extraordinary life—to radically change your surroundings by bringing God's Imperial Rule on the earth. Time is short...make the most of every opportunity you have. In an attitude of love, carry out the specific task you've been given. As salt and light, you will please the Lord and be prepared when He comes.

Voice of the Ages

"Without expectation, do something for love itself, not for what you may receive. *Love in action* is what gives us *grace*. We have been created for greater things—to love and to be loved.

Open your hearts to the love God instills... God loves you tenderly. What He gives you is not to be kept under lock and key but to be *shared*.

Yesterday is gone. Tomorrow has not yet come. We have only today. *Let us begin*."

—**Mother Teresa**[6]

UNVEIL YOUR HERO

A stay-at-home mom takes on her call of empowering her children to greatness—allowing them from a young age to be themselves, think creatively, and be influencers to those around them.

Teri is raising world changers..

Journal Your Journey

" To live in the ability of grace, through faith, motivated by *compassion* and sincere *love* will avail much in the eyes of God and men. May you be one of the extraordinary ones of our generation! You're needed to arise, shine, and reveal His Imperial Rule and glorious reign. "

JOHN BEVERE
adapted from chapter 17

EYE-OPENERS

One word from God, spoken into your spirit, is more life-changing than the knowledge received from thousands of books. What transforming truths is the Holy Spirit speaking to you?

REVOLUTIONARY YOU

As a son or daughter of the Most High, you have been called to rule and reign on earth. What new goals do you sense you must set in place to more effectively execute God's authority?

PRAYER

Father, I pray that Your love in me will overflow more and more to others, and at the same time I keep on growing in spiritual insight and knowledge of You. May I and all believers always see clearly the difference between right and wrong and remain inwardly clean, so that we don't bring dishonor to Your name. Take all that I have studied through this curriculum and help me apply it in my daily life so I can truly live **extraordinarily** *from now until the time Jesus returns...in His name, Amen!*

SALT & LIGHT

> Let me tell you why you are here. You're here to be **salt**-seasoning that brings out the God-flavors of this earth. If you lose your saltiness, how will people taste godliness? ...Here's another way to put it: You're here to be **light**, bringing out the God-colors in the world. God is not a secret to be kept. We're going public with this, as public as a city on a hill.
> —Matthew 5:13-14 The Message

Salt and light...that's what Jesus calls us. To understand what He is saying, contemplate the purposes for both of these everyday items.

What is salt used for? The first use that comes to mind is *adding flavor* to food. Sprinkling a little salt into the hot stew on your stove makes the flavors mix and come alive. Another use for salt, especially in Jesus' day, was to *preserve* food from decaying. Salt is also used for *medicinal* purposes, to purify and bring healing to the body.

As a believer, God has called **you** to *add flavor* to the world around you—to enhance and bring out the wonderful savor of the Savior. He wants people to truly "taste and see that the Lord is good" and come alive in Him (Psalm 34:8). As salt, God also has prepared and positioned you to *preserve* the lives of the people around you from spiritual decay. For those who are sick with sin, your life is to be the *medicine* that brings cleansing and healing to their lives.

In what specific ways are you acting as *salt* in the society that surrounds you? How does your "salty" life make others thirst for Jesus, the Living Water?

_____

_____

_____

Check out Colossians 4:5-6.

Heaven's APPEAL

You are the world's **light**—a city on a hill, glowing in the night for all to see. Don't hide your light! Let it shine for all; let your good deeds *glow* for all to see, so that they will praise your heavenly Father.

—Matthew 5:14-16 TLB

Jesus also calls us "light." What would life be like without light? Dark. The first and most obvious benefit of light is that it gives us the *ability to see* clearly and vividly the world around us, including the people we cherish dearly. Light is also a *source of life* itself. Light from the sun provides the energy needed for all vegetation to grow and produce food, not to mention the warmth it brings for life to exist.

Interestingly, the pupils of our eyes are designed to respond to light—not darkness. In darkness, they will dilate, opening larger and larger, searching for every ounce of light they can take in. Keep in mind, "Your eye is a *lamp* for your body. A pure eye lets *sunshine* into your soul" (Matthew 6:22 NLT).

In the midst of the darkening world we live in, there are people all around us whose eyes are dilating to take in the divine light of Jesus Christ. Whether they know it or not, they are desperately looking for illumination as to which path to take—their spirit and soul are yearning for the warm sunshine of the Son to bring life to their being. The question is: Are they receiving this life-giving Light from you?

In what specific ways do you believe your life is a *light* to those living around you? How can you enhance the radiance you are emitting?

_____

_____

_____

_____

_____

_____

Heaven's APPEAL

For once you were darkness, but now **you are light** in the Lord; walk as children of Light [lead the lives of those native-born to the Light].

—Ephesians 5:8 AMP

Check out 1 Peter 2:11-12; Titus 2:7-8; 3:8.

So how can you, in a practical way, effectively be salt and light to those around you? The avenue of opportunity is to be *personally involved* in their lives. Through **relationships** with people in their everyday existence, we affect them and earn the right to speak the truth in love. Check out these startling statistics that hammer home the power of the personal touch:

Eighty percent of all the people who have come forward to receive Christ during a Billy Graham crusade were brought by a *friend* or *relative*. That is the figure Billy Graham's Association has determined through decades of research. Elmer Towns affirms this statistic with his own research. Dr. Towns has been taking a personal survey in his seminars for 12 years all across America. The results of these surveys reveal the following about how people have come to Christ: 2 percent through non-personal advertising (TV, radio, literature, etc.), 6 percent because of the personal influence of a pastor, 6 percent through the intentional evangelistic efforts of a church, and *86 percent* found Jesus as a result of a friend or relative. Unfortunately, the church appears to be missing this important truth, because a recent Gallup poll showed that 63 percent of unchurched Americans have *not* been invited to church by their friends. Slick marketing will never replace a **personal relationship**.[7]

As we live in relationship with God, our very lives act as *salt* and *light* to others. The choices we make day in and day out, and the results they bring, preach volumes to others before a word is ever spoken.

It is the witness of our life that opens the door to the witness of our lips. Therefore, we must also be ready to share the Gospel message in a fresh, clear, relevant way at a moment's notice to anyone the Lord brings across our path. Read 1 Peter 3:15 and write how you are challenged by it.

_____

_____

_____

_____

Also **check out** 2 Timothy 2:15; 4:2.

What else can you do to act as salt and light? **Pray.** Prayer paves the way for God to move in the lives of the lost and gives you a heart of compassion to see them saved. Here are some specific points of prayer to consider as you pray for the salvation of your family and friends:

Lord, in Your mercy, I ask You to...
In prayer, speak a friend or family member's name in each blank.

Open the blind eyes and deaf ears of _____ so he/she can see and hear the truth; give him/her the measure of faith he/she needs to believe and receive Christ as his/her Savior and Lord.

Create the circumstances and situations necessary that will soften _____ heart and cause him/her to come (or return) to You.

Surround _____ with people (including me) who will show him/her Christ in their lives and speak the truth in love to him/her at the right time, in the right way.

Reveal Yourself to _____ through people, TV, radio, Internet, books, and anything else You know will grab his/her attention.

Show _____ that You are real, that You love him/her intensely, and that he/she cannot live without You...in Jesus' name, Amen!

FOR FURTHER STUDY

RULING WITH CHRIST
    Luke 22:28-30
    2 Timothy 2:11-13
    Revelation 1:5-6; 3:21

THE NEED FOR LOVE
    Ephesians 4:15-16; 5:1-2
    Colossians 3:12-14
    1 John 4:7-21

EXPERIENCING PEACE
    Psalm 4:8; 29:11; 119:165
    Isaiah 26:3
    Matthew 11:28-30
    John 14:27; 16:33

REMAIN IN THE LIGHT
    John 8:12
    2 Corinthians 4:6
    Ephesians 5:13-14
    1 John 1:5-7

1. Adapted from *Noah Webster's First Edition of an American Dictionary of the English Language* (1828), Republished in facsimile edition by Foundation for American Christian Education (San Francisco, CA, 1995). 2. *Fast Break, Five-Minute Devotions to Start Your Day* (St. San Luis Obispo, CA: Parable, 2007) Day 57. 3. John Hudson Tiner, *For Those Who Dare: 101 Great Christians and How They Changed the World* (Green Forest, AR: Master Books, Inc., 2002) adapted from pp.20-22; 84-86; 187-189; 236-237. 4. See note 2, Day 123. 5. Frances J. Roberts, *Come Away My Beloved* (Ojai, CA: King's Farspan, Inc., 1973) p. 125. 6. Quotes by Mother Theresa (http://dailychristianquote. com/dcqteresa.html, retrieved 6/24/09). 7. Raymond McHenry, *McHenry's Quips, Quotes & Other Notes* (Peabody MA: Hendrickson Publishers, Inc., 2004), adapted from pp. 177-178.

NOTES

NOTES

JOIN OVER **300,000 PEOPLE** WHOSE LIVES HAVE BEEN TRANSFORMED BY OUR CURRICULUMS.

Extraordinary
CURRICULUM

The *Extraordinary* Curriculum is an extensive journey with 12 video and audio sessions, a thought-provoking devotional workbook, and a hardcover book. As each session builds, you will be positioned to step into the unknown and embrace your divine empowerment.

INCLUDES:

- 12 30-MINUTE VIDEO SESSIONS ON 4 DVDS
- 12 30-MINUTE AUDIO SESSIONS ON 6 CDS
- HARDCOVER BOOK
- DEVOTIONAL WORKBOOK
- PROMOTIONAL MATERIALS

BREAKING INTIMIDATION
CURRICULUM

Everyone has been intimidated at some point in life. Do you really know why it happened or how to keep it from happening again? John Bevere exposes the root of intimidation, challenges you to break its fearful grip, and teaches you to release God's gifts and establish His dominion in your life.

INCLUDES:

- EIGHT 30-MINUTE VIDEO SESSIONS ON 3 DVDS
- EIGHT 30-MINUTE AUDIO SESSIONS ON 4 CDS
- BREAKING INTIMIDATION BOOK
- DEVOTIONAL WORKBOOK
- PROMOTIONAL MATERIALS

INCLUDES:

- 12 30-MINUTE VIDEO LESSONS ON 4 DVDS
- 12 30-MINUTE AUDIO LESSONS ON 6 CDS
- HONOR'S REWARD HARDCOVER BOOK
- DEVOTIONAL WORKBOOK
- PROMOTIONAL MATERIALS

HONOR'S REWARD
CURRICULUM

This curriculum will unveil the power and truth of an often overlooked principle–Honor. If you understand the vital role of this virtue, you will attract blessing both now and for eternity. This insightful message teaches you how to extend honor to your Creator, family members, authorities and those who surround your world.

DRIVEN *by* Eternity
CURRICULUM

Making Your Life Count Today & Forever

We were made for eternity. This life on earth is but a vapor. Yet too many live as though there is nothing on the other side. Scriptural laws and principles may be applied to achieve success on earth, but are we prepared for eternity? This power-packed teaching, including an allegory on the Kingdom of Affabel, will help you understand that the choices you make today will determine how you spend eternity.

INCLUDES:

- 12 40-MINUTE VIDEO LESSONS ON 4 DVDS
- DRIVEN BY ETERNITY HARDCOVER BOOK
- HARDCOVER DEVOTIONAL WORKBOOK
- AFFABEL AUDIO THEATER

THE BAIT OF SATAN

CURRICULUM

Jesus said, "It's impossible that no offenses will come."
–Luke 17:1

A most crucial message for believers in this hour.

"This message is possibly the most important confrontation with truth you'll encounter in your lifetime. The issue of offense – the very core of *The Bait of Satan* – is often the most difficult obstacle an individual must face and overcome."
– John Bevere

INCLUDES:
- 12 30-MINUTE VIDEO LESSONS ON 4 DVDs
- 12 30-MINUTE AUDIO LESSONS ON 6 CDs
- BEST-SELLING BOOK THE BAIT OF SATAN
- DEVOTIONAL WORKBOOK
- PROMOTIONAL MATERIALS

A HEART ABLAZE

CURRICULUM

Jesus has never accepted lukewarmness. Rather, He calls for passion! This message will challenge you to exchange a mediocre relationship with God for a vibrant, fiery one.

INCLUDES:
- 12 30-MINUTE VIDEO LESSONS ON 4 DVDs
- 12 30-MINUTE AUDIO LESSONS ON 6 CDs
- A HEART ABLAZE BEST-SELLING BOOK
- DEVOTIONAL WORKBOOK
- PROMOTIONAL MATERIALS

INCLUDES:
- 12 30-MINUTE VIDEO LESSONS ON 4 DVDs
- 12 30-MINUTE AUDIO LESSONS ON 6 CDs
- BEST-SELLING BOOK UNDER COVER
- DEVOTIONAL WORKBOOK
- PROMOTIONAL MATERIALS

UNDER COVER

CURRICULUM

Under the shadow of the Almighty, there is liberty, provision and protection. Unfortunately, many don't understand how to find this secret place. In this curriculum you will learn how biblical submission differs from obedience. You will also learn the distinction between direct and delegated authority and how to respond to and overcome unfair treatment.

DRAWING NEAR

CURRICULUM

Drawing extensively from his own journey, John has specially written and prepared this *Drawing Near* message to lead you into times of private and intimate communion with God Himself. This devotional kit acts as a treasure map, guiding you around potential pitfalls and breaking through personal barriers leading you into new and glorious realms of a lifelong adventure with God!

INCLUDES:
- 12 30-MINUTE VIDEO LESSONS ON 4 DVDs
- BEST-SELLING BOOK DRAWING NEAR
- 84-DAY DEVOTIONAL
- WORKBOOK

RESCUED

2 hours on 2 CDs · AUDIO THEATER

From the
novel
Rescued

Starring:
Roma Downey from *Touched by an Angel*
John Rhys-Davies from *The Lord of the Rings*
Marisol Nichols from the hit TV show *24*

A trapped father. A desperate son. A clock ticking down toward certain death and a fate even more horrible still...
For Alan Rockaway, his teenaged son Jeff, and his new bride Jenny, it's been little more than a leisurely end to a weeklong cruise...

a horrifying crash and even more, a plunge toward the unknown...Everything Alan has assumed about himself is flipped upside down. In the ultimate rescue operation, life or death is just the beginning!

AFFABEL

WINDOW of ETERNITY

2.5 hours on 4 CDs

FEATURING JOHN RHYS-DAVIES
AND A CAST OF HOLLYWOOD ACTORS

AN EPIC AUDIO THEATER PORTRAYING THE REALITY OF THE JUDGMENT SEAT OF CHRIST. GET READY TO BE CHANGED FOREVER...AND PREPARE FOR ETERNITY!

This audio dramatization, taken from John Bevere's book, *Driven by Eternity*, will capture your heart and soul as you experience life on "the other side" where eternity is brought into the present and all must stand before the Great King and Judge. Be prepared for a roller coaster ride of joy, sorrow, astonishment, and revelation as lifelong rewards are bestowed on some while others are bound hand and foot and cast into outer darkness by the Royal Guard!

BOOKS BY JOHN

The Bait of Satan
Breaking Intimidation
Drawing Near
Driven by Eternity
Enemy Access Denied
Extraordinary
The Fear of the Lord
A Heart Ablaze

Honor's Reward
How to Respond When You Feel Mistreated
Rescued
Thus Saith the Lord
Under Cover
Victory in the Wilderness
The Voice of One Crying

life-transforming truth.
Messenger International.

Messenger International, founded by John and Lisa Bevere, imparts the fear of the Lord while inspiring freedom through the spoken and written Word to release people into their fulfilled lives in Christ.

UNITED STATES
P.O. Box 888
Palmer Lake, CO
80133-0888
800-648-1477 (US & Canada)
Tel: 719-487-3000
mail@MessengerInternational.org

AUSTRALIA
Rouse Hill Town Centre
P.O. Box 6444
Rouse Hill NSW 2155
In AUS: 1-300-650-577
Tel: +61 2 9679 4900
aus@MessengerInternational.org

EUROPE
P.O. Box 1066
Hemel, Hempstead HP2 7GQ
United Kingdom
In UK: 0800 9808 933
Tel: +44 1442 288 531
europe@MessengerInternational.org

The Messenger television program broadcasts in over 200 countries including the U.S. on GOD TV, the Australian Christian Channel and the New Life Channel in Russia.
Please check your local listings for day and time.

www.MessengerInternational.org